Road Atlas

2017 MIDSIZE

CONTENTS

TRAVEL INFORMATION

Best of the Road® Trips ii-xii
Our editor's five favorite road trips from our Best of the Road® collection.

Tourism Contacts xiii
Phone numbers and websites for tourism information in each state and province.

Road Construction and Road Conditions Resources xiv-xv
Numbers to call and websites to visit for road information in each state and province.

Hotel Resources 81

Mileage Chart 82
Driving distances between 77 North American cities.

Mileage and Driving Times Map inside back cover
Distances and driving times between over a hundred North American cities and national parks.

MAPS

Map legend inside front cover

United States overview map 2-3

U.S. states 4-53

Canada overview map 54-55

Canadian provinces 56-63

Mexico overview map and Puerto Rico 64

U.S. and Canadian cities 65-80

Published and printed in U.S.A.

For licensing information and copyright permissions, contact us at permissions@randmcnally.com

If you have a comment, suggestion, or even a compliment, please visit us at randmcnally.com/contact
or write to:
Rand McNally Consumer Affairs
P.O. Box 7600
Chicago, Illinois 60680-9915

1 2 3 VE 17 16

Certified Chain of Custody
Promoting Sustainable Forestry
www.sfiprogram.org
SFI-00993

Best of the Road® Trips

If you're like us, you love road trips. Here are some favorites from our Best of the Road collection. They follow scenic routes along stretches of coastline, both east and west; to forests and mountains; and through small towns and big cities.

Duquesne Incline, Pittsburgh

Western Pennsylvania Town & Country

Ohiopyle State Park

From Pittsburgh's steel heritage to Fallingwater's architectural wonder to Gettysburg's Civil War history, a trip through western Pennsylvania will satisfy your craving for urban adventure, natural serenity, and Americana in one succinct weekend.

Outside Pittsburgh city limits, the scenery quickly changes to tree-lined streets, town squares, and state routes that have become hallmarks of rural Pennsylvania. Along the way you can immerse yourself in Colonial history as well as that of the Civil War. And, at a national memorial

in a field in Stoystown, you can also pay homage to some of the victims of the tragic events on September 11, 2001.

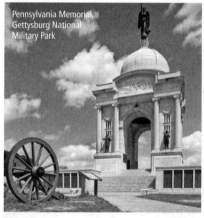
Pennsylvania Memorial, Gettysburg National Military Park

Distance: 218 miles point to point.

Type of Trip: Weekend Getaway; RV; Arts & Culture, History and Heritage, Sports Fans.

Must Buy: Steelers fans should pick up an iconic Terrible Towel. Gettysburg finds include Civil War memorabilia ranging from authentic antiques to kitsch replicas. Throughout the region, look for folk art inspired by Pennsylvania Dutch and Amish designs.

Must See: Andy Warhol Museum, Duquesne Incline, Fallingwater, Flight 93 National Memorial, Gettysburg National Military Site.

Worth Noting: Pittsburgh offers three distinct shopping areas: the South Side, with its artsy vibe; the Strip District, with its wholesale and ethnic markets; and Shadyside, with its upscale shops. Restaurants, bars, and concert venues also make these popular destinations for a night out. In Gettysburg, the antiques shops lining Steinwehr Avenue make for a shopping experience that's more like a scavenger hunt.

Travel Tips: Take this trip in the fall to see spectacular displays of autumnal colors.

Atlas map F-2, p. 44

Western Pennsylvania
Town & Country

Pittsburgh

Andy Warhol Museum. Each floor of this seven-story building follows a decade of the life and art of Andy Warhol, who was born in Pittsburgh in 1928. In addition to the well-known Pop Art collection (those Campbell's soup cans) and portraits (Elvis, Marilyn, Jackie O), the museum has about a half-million bits of ephemera: from Warhol's party invitations and scrapbooks to his trademark silver-white wigs. The café is a convenient place for lunch. *117 Sandusky St., (412) 237-8300, www.warhol.org.*

Duquesne Incline. It was built to haul freight and passengers up Mount Washington, and today its century-old, fully restored wooden cable cars carry commuters as well as visitors. Don't miss the views from the Upper Station observation deck or from one of the restaurants along Grandview Avenue. There's free parking across the street from the Lower Station. *1197 W. Carson St., (412) 381-1665, www.duquesneincline.org.*

Station Square. This 52-acre complex on the Monongahela River was once the hub of the Pittsburgh and Lake Erie Railroad. Some of the boxcars have been converted into shops, and the station houses the Grand Concourse restaurant. There are also more than 40 shops and 20 restaurants, a riverboat cruise line, amusements, entertainment venues, and nightclubs. Plus, it's a convenient 5-minute walk from the heart of Pittsburgh. *125 W. Station Square Dr., (412) 261-2811, www.stationsquare.com.*

Latrobe

Steelers Training Camp. Grab your Terrible Towel and head to St. Vincent College, the summer retreat and training ground of the Pittsburgh Steelers.

(Coincidentally, it's the alma mater of team co-owner Art Rooney, Jr.) The camp is open to the public and offers Steelers history and merchandise as well as daily fan activities such as field-goal kicks and quarterback tosses. *300 Fraser Purchase Rd., (412) 432-7800, www.steelers.com/schedule-and-events.*

Mill Run

Fallingwater. Designed by Frank Lloyd Wright in 1935 for the Kaufmanns, the prominent Pittsburgh family that owned Kaufmann's department store, this house generated national attention when it appeared on the cover of *Time* magazine in January 1938. It's built on cantilevers over a 30-foot waterfall, so it becomes one with its natural setting. It served as a summer retreat until 1963, when Edgar Kaufmann Jr. gave the home to the Western Pennsylvania Conservancy. It's the only Wright-designed house open to the public with its original furnishings, artwork, and setting intact; it's now a National Historic Landmark. (Advance tickets recommended.) *1491 Mill Run Rd., (724) 329-8501, www.fallingwater.org.*

Statue of General Gouverneur Kemble Warren at Little Round Top, Gettysburg National Military Park

Stoystown

Flight 93 National Memorial. On Tuesday morning, September 11, 2001, United Airlines Flight 93 was hijacked. Realizing the goal was to destroy the U.S. Capitol, the 40 passengers and crew devised a plan to crash the plane into a field before it reached Washington. The field is now home to a 2,200-acre National Park Site, where a Wall of Names honors those aboard the flight and marks a portion of the flight path. A hemlock grove damaged by the crash has been replanted with trees, wildflowers, and native grasses. The mile-wide Field of Honor is viewable from the crash site. There's also a Visitor Center and a Learning Center. *6424 Lincoln Hwy., (814) 893-6322, www.nps.gov.*

Gettysburg

Gettysburg National Military Park and Cemetery. Portions of the Gettysburg battlefield are much as they were that fateful July day in 1863. You can explore more than 1,300 monuments along 40 miles of scenic roadways on bus tours or self-guided drives. The National Park Service Museum and Visitor Center has a huge collection of Civil War relics, interactive exhibits, a 22-minute film, and the fully restored Gettysburg Cyclorama mural. There's also a bookstore, a café that serves Civil War–era cuisine, a campground, and several miles of bike paths and hiking or bridle trails. The adjoining, 17-acre Gettysburg National Cemetery is the final resting place of more than 6,000 soldiers, including 3,512 from the Civil War. This is also where President Lincoln delivered his famous address. *1195 Baltimore Pike (Rte. 97), (717) 334-1124, www.nps.gov/gett.*

Fallingwater

Historic Georgia: In & Around Savannah

Forsyth Park, Savannah

This is the perfect weekend escape for, well, anyone: couples, families, best friends, beach lovers, history buffs. Although it takes you on side trips south and east of Savannah, it centers on the city's 2.2-square-mile Historic District. Amid streets lined with 18th- and 19th-century buildings and trees draped in Spanish moss, you truly feel transported back in time.

The city that was the only one to survive General Sherman's March to the Sea was founded in 1733 and has sites dating from the Colonial and Federal periods as well as those related to the Civil War and Underground Railway. Savannah is also a bustling port, so be sure to see it from the water aboard a riverboat.

Distance: 45 miles point to point (Savannah to Tybee Island via sights to the south); 36 miles point to point (Savannah to Tybee Island).

Type of Trip: Weekend Getaway; Arts & Culture, History & Heritage, Picture Perfect.

Must Buy: Anything from the River Street complex's boutiques, galleries, and studios. Also, pottery, jewelry, handbags, clothes, and other items crafted by Savannah College of Art and Design (SCAD) students and sold at **shopSCAD** (340 Bull St., 912/525-5180).

Must See: Telfair Museums, Forsyth Park, Pin Point Heritage Museum, Tybee Island.

Worth Noting: This town is up for a good time, with plenty of nightspots that you can hop between, drink in hand (just put it in a plastic cup). "Midnight" the Book and Movie Tour led by **Savannah Heritage Tour** (912/224-8365, www.savannahheritagetour.com) hits all the hot spots from John Berendt's best-selling book, *Midnight in the Garden of Good and Evil.*

Travel Tips: Park the car and walk, particularly in the Historic District, bordered by the Savannah River to the north, Gwinnett Street to the south, Martin Luther King, Jr. Boulevard to the west, and Broad Street to the east. If you get tired, hail one of the ubiquitous pedicabs.

Atlas map F-7, p. 15

Savannah

Savannah History Museum. Housed in a converted railway station in Tricentennial Park, this museum offers a great introduction to the city's rich legacy. Exhibits highlight English settlement in 1733, the 1779 Siege of Savannah, the Civil War, the Industrial Revolution, and Savannah's arts scene. Across the street, Battlefield Memorial Park honors those who fought in the American Revolution's second-bloodiest battle. The site is also home to the Georgia State Railroad Museum and the **Savannah Children's Museum** (912/651-4292). *303 Martin Luther King, Jr. Blvd., (912) 651-6825, www.chsgeorgia.org.*

Green-Meldrim House. Among the noteworthy Historic District buildings you can tour is the 1850 Green-Meldrim House, where General William Tecumseh Sherman stayed during Union occupation on the March to the Sea. Sherman considered Savannah too pretty to burn. Instead, he sent a letter to Abraham Lincoln giving him the city as a Christmas gift in 1864. *14 W. Macon St., Madison Sq., (912) 233-3845, www.stjohnssav.org.*

Forsyth Park. The southern edge of the Historic District is home to a 30-acre park with one of Savannah's most photographed attractions—the white, two-tiered, cast-iron fountain made famous in *Midnight in the Garden of Good and Evil*. Adults love the peacefulness of the park; kids love the open space. *Drayton St., (912) 651-6610, visithistoricsavannah.com/forsyth-park.*

Telfair Museums. Founded in 1883, the South's oldest art museum has three buildings, each containing works that correspond to the era in which it was built. Telfair Academy is home to 19th- and 20th-century American and European art; the Owens-Thomas House has a collection of late 18th- to early 19th-century decorative arts and an exhibit featuring an intact urban slave quarters; and the contemporary Jepson Center has the Glass House and the Sculpture Terrace. Another highlight is Sylvia Shaw Judson's *Bird Girl*, a statue made famous on the cover of *Midnight in the Garden of Good and Evil*. *121 Barnard St., (912) 790-8800, www.telfair.org.*

Pin Point

Pin Point Heritage Museum. About 11 miles southeast of downtown Savannah, Pin Point is one of the Georgia coast's few remaining traditional Gullah-Geechee communities, where residents are descendants of first-generation freed slaves. From 1926 until 1985, A.S. Varn & Son Oyster Seafood Factory was the area's main employer. Its closure threatened not only the community but also a way of life. This museum, however, helps to preserve the area's unique culture. *9924 Pin Point Ave., (912) 667-9176, www.pinpointheritagemuseum.com.*

Skidaway Island

Skidaway Island State Park. You can follow stretches of the Colonial Coast Birding Trail, along which more than 300 species have been spotted, through this 588-acre site about 13 miles southeast of downtown Savannah. It's also home to the 1-mile Sandpiper and 3-mile Big Ferry trails as well as a boardwalk that leads to a wildlife observation tower. An interpretive center has reference materials and ranger programs. *52 Diamond Causeway, (912) 598-2300, www.gastateparks.org/SkidawayIsland.*

Isle of Hope

Wormsloe State Historic Site. In the 1730s, colonist Noble Jones carved out an impressive plantation. Today, a 1.5-mile, oak-lined avenue leads to what's left of the house, which remained in the Jones family until 1973. Like many residences along the Georgia and South Carolina coast, it was a "tabby house," built using cement that's a mixture of sand, water, lime, wood ash, and oyster shells. The on-site museum has excavated artifacts and a short film; the Colonial Life Area often has costumed docents demonstrating period crafts and trades. *7601 Skidaway Rd., (912) 353-3023, www.gastateparks.org/Wormsloe.*

Fort Pulaski

Fort Pulaski National Monument. Although it predates the Civil War, this fort is most famous for a 30-hour 1862 bombardment that resulted in Union forces seizing it from the Confederates. The visitors center has historical exhibits, a bookstore, and a gift shop. Ranger-led walks through the fort's interior are available. *U.S. Hwy. 80 E., (912) 786-5787, www.nps.gov/fopu.*

Tybee Island

Tybee Light Station and Museum. Given its 3-mile strand of gorgeous white sand and a location just 18 miles east of Hostess City, this barrier island serves as Savannah's public beach. The island is also home to Georgia's oldest (circa 1732) and tallest lighthouse, **Tybee Light Station and Museum** (30 Meddin Ave., 912/786-5801, www.tybeelighthouse.org). Climb the tower's 178 steps for a view of the entire island. *802 1st St., (877) 344-3361, tybeeisland.com.*

Savannah

Tybee Island

Missouri Family Fun & Fine Fiddling

Ozark Mountain fall scenery

The middle of Missouri offers plenty of family fun, down-home food, and lake and Ozark Mountain scenery. And, of course there's Branson, the hub for fine music—on the fiddle and other instruments. In Jefferson City, the majesty of the Missouri River and its tree-lined bluffs is captivating, and so is the capitol itself.

South of the state capital is the Lake of the Ozarks, where you can swim, paddle, fish, or just relax waterside. The region also has several caves to explore and a Civil War battlefield to tour. Highway 65 south takes you to the Tri-Lakes Area (Table Rock Lake, Lake Taneycomo, and Bull Shoals Lake) and Branson, playgrounds for the child in everyone.

Atlas map D-5, p. 28

Distance: 210 miles point to point.

Type of Trip: Weekend Getaway; Arts & Music, Great Outdoors, History & Heritage, Small Town Gems.

Must Buy: Tickets to at least one Branson show. Find out what's going on in the 50-plus theaters through the **Branson Tourism Center** (220 Branson Hills Pkwy., 800/785-1550, www.bransontourismcenter.com), which sells tickets and has information on all kinds of lodging, dining, and other packages.

Must See: Missouri State Penitentiary & Museum, Fantastic Caverns, Wilson's Creek National Battlefield, Silver Dollar City.

Worth Noting: South and west of Jefferson City, more than a dozen vineyards and wineries are part of the officially designated Ozark Mountain American Viticultural Area. **The Missouri Wine and Grape Board** (missouriwine.org) has information on this and other state viticulture areas; its website also has a winery-tour planning tool. To this we say, "Prost!"

Travel Tips: To lengthen this trip, consider adding on a visit to St. Louis. From Jefferson City, it's just a 2-hour, 130-mile drive, most of it along I-70, to the Gateway to the West. You could also readily combine this trip with one to Arkansas. Branson is a mere 50 miles northeast of Eureka Springs.

Missouri Family Fun & Fine Fiddling

Showboat *Branson Belle* paddle-wheeler

Jefferson City

Missouri State Capitol & Museum. The third Missouri State Capitol on this downtown site was modeled after the U.S. Capitol, built of Missouri-quarried marble, and completed in 1917. A tour of its grounds, interior, and on-site state history museum provides a great overview of both Missouri and Jefferson City. Admission is free, so are the 45-minute guided tours, which take place on each hour (except for noon) Monday through Saturday 9–4 and Sunday at 10, 11, 2, and 3. *201 W. Capitol Ave., (573) 751-2854 or (573) 751-4127 (tour info), mostateparks.com.*

Jefferson Landing State Historic Site. The Lohman Building, a one-time warehouse, is set up just as it would have been in the days when river boats and, later, the railroads, stopped here. The Rozier Gallery, inside the landing's Union Hotel, has rotating exhibits of memorabilia, photographs, and art. Admission to the site is free. *100 Jefferson St., (573) 751-2854, mostateparks.com.*

Missouri State Penitentiary & Museum. Before being decommissioned in 2004, this was the oldest continuously operating prison west of the Mississippi. In 1836, when it opened, the Battle of the Alamo was going on, and Andrew Jackson was in his second term. By the time Alcatraz began accepting prisoners, MSP was 100 years old—and well on its way to infamy. Buy advance tickets for the history, ghost, and other prison tours, and be sure to visit the nearby **Missouri State Penitentiary Museum** (100 High Street), where admission is free. *115 Lafayette St., (866) 998-6998, www. missouripentours.com.*

Lake of the Ozarks Area

Lake of the Ozarks State Park & Ozark Cavern. Missouri's largest state park comprises 17,626 acres. It has 89 miles of shoreline, two swimming beaches, horseback riding, and more than 10 developed trails—one of which, the Ozarks Aquatic Trail, is designed for boaters, with 14 designated buoy stops along the shore. Take time for a guided tour of the park-operated Ozark Caverns, where a highlight is the unusual Angel Showers formation. *403 Hwy. 134, Kaiser, (573) 348-2694, mostateparks.com.*

Springfield

Fantastic Caverns. The temperature in Fantastic Caverns is a constant 60 degrees, and the trip through them is easy because all the work is done by a Jeep-drawn tram. Along the way, you'll see limestone stalactites, stalagmites, and other formations. You'll learn about cavern inhabitants, like the blind Ozarks cave fish, and past cavern uses—as a place to grow mushrooms, a fallout shelter, and a music hall. *4872 N. Farm Rd. 125, (417) 833-2010, www.fantasticcaverns.com.*

Republic

Wilson's Creek National Battlefield. The first major Civil War battle west of the Mississippi River claimed the life of Nathaniel Lyon, the first Union general to die in the conflict. Although it was considered a Confederate victory, they suffered heavy losses and were prevented from making inroads into Missouri. The land around the so-called Bloody Hill remains much as it was when the battle raged here on August 10, 1861. The visitors center has military exhibits and a well-stocked bookstore. You can take a self- or cell-phone-guided 4.9-mile driving tour, featuring 8 interpretive sites, or explore on foot along one of 5 short trails off the tour road. *6424 W. Farm Rd. 182, (417) 732-2662, ext. 227, www.nps.gov/wicr.*

Branson

Silver Dollar City. Folksy, 1880s-themed Silver Dollar City, 5 miles west of Branson off Highway 76, emphasizes Ozark crafts and culture. The entertainment complex has more than 40 rides; historic structures like a 19th-century homestead, school, and church; and a colony of 100 resident artisans. Affiliated with Silver Dollar City are the White Water Park, with its watery rides and slides, and the 278-foot *Branson Belle* paddle-wheeler, which sails from the shop-lined boardwalk at White River Landing, just south of Branson. *399 Silver Dollar City Pkwy., (800) 475-9370, www. silverdollarcity.com.*

Dick's Old Time 5&10. With an inventory of 50,000 items—give or take—you could explore this store for hours. Shelves are packed with toys, gifts, housewares, and hardware. If you're not a collector, you might just become one after seeing the aviation, train, sports, and other memorabilia. And it's hard to resist picking up a few sweets in the old-time candy aisle. *103 W. Main St., (417) 334-2410, dicksoldtime5and10.com.*

Silver Dollar City

Arkansas Springs Eternal

Hot Springs National Park

This trip starts and ends in towns known for their curative waters. In the hillside resort of Eureka Springs, the Victorian architecture is so well preserved that the entire downtown district is on the National Register of Historic Places. There are more than 60 springs in the town itself, including the Blue, Basin, Grotto, and Crescent.

To the south and east is Hot Springs, whose thermal waters put it on the map first as a healing center, then as a national park, and then as a gangster getaway.

There's a lot of colorful history in and between these communities. And then there's all that nature along and through swatches of the million-acre Ozark National Forest and the 1.8-million-acre Ouachita National Forest.

Atlas map A-2, p. 7

Distance: 280 miles point to point.

Type of Trip: Weekend Getaway; Arts & Culture, Great Outdoors, Quirky & Oddball, Small Town Gems.

Must Buy: Eureka Springs is home to hundreds of artists and artisans, so a handcrafted work from here is a must. Hot Springs also has its share of craftspeople, particularly potters.

Must See: Thorncrown Chapel, Crystal Bridges Museum, Fordyce Bathhouse in Hot Springs National Park, the Gangster Museum of America.

Worth Noting: The main office of Ozark National Forest is in Russellville, 85 miles east of Fort Smith and 72 miles north of Hot Springs. That for Ouachita National Forest is in Hot Springs. Throughout both forests there are numerous ranger stations, recreation areas, and tent and RV campgrounds, both rustic and developed.

Travel Tips: This trip picks up just about where the Missouri Family Fun and Fine Fiddling trip leaves off. You can also follow the 19-mile Pig Trail Scenic Byway as well as segments of the Ozark Highlands Scenic Byway, Arkansas Scenic 7 Byway, and Talimena Scenic Byway.

Fort Smith

Eureka Springs

Eureka Springs Tram Tours. Narrated, 90-minute tours take you up and down the town's hilly streets lined with always-stately and often-colorful Victorian architecture. Stops include the Crescent Hotel and Grotto Spring. Tours often sell out; reserve ahead. *137 W. Van Buren St., (800) 386-8711, www.eurekaspringstramtours.com.*

Quicksilver Gallery. This two-floor shop sells works by about 120 of the more than 200 working artists, artisans, and craftspeople that call this historic town home. *73 Spring St., (479) 253-7679, quicksilvergallery.com.*

Thorncrown Chapel. The gabled, 48-foot-high, sky-lighted roof seems to balance atop a frame of pine columns and latticework beams. The walls are made of glass—6,000 square feet of it. The result is a soaring, light-filled Ozark Gothic building that's perfectly at home amid the surrounding hardwood forest. *12968 Hwy. 62 W., (479) 253-7401, www.thorncrown.com.*

Bentonville

Crystal Bridges Museum of American Art. Alice Walton, longtime art collector and daughter of the Walmart founder, was instrumental in establishing this truly special place. In the sleek, interconnected pavilions, the American art–filled galleries are as compelling as the wooded and watery views through the window-lined corridors. The collection includes works by Winslow Homer, John Singer Sargent, Georgia O'Keeffe, Edward Hopper, and Norman Rockwell. In addition to taking in the art, you can hike or bike the 120-acre site along seven short trails. *600 Museum Way, (479) 418-5700, crystalbridges.org.*

Fort Smith

Fort Smith National Historic Site. Established in 1817 to protect the area's few settlers, Fort Smith was briefly abandoned and later rebuilt to serve as a military supply depot. In 1872, it was transformed from fort to court as an attempt to instill order in what was still a rough-and-tumble, far western outpost. Exhibits in several restored buildings cover the military; area outlaws; the U.S. Marshal Service; and the Trail of Tears, an 1838–39 forced march west during which thousands of Native Americans died. Be sure to see the courthouse's basement jail; the reproduction gallows; and the displays of handcuffs, leg irons, and guns—all testaments to life on the edge of lawlessness. *301 Parker Ave., (479) 783-3961, www.nps.gov/fosm.*

Fort Smith Museum of History. Fascinating exhibits take you from Fort Smith's days as a frontier town in Indian Territory to its post–Civil War federal court period and beyond. Highlights include a re-creation of the courtroom presided over by Judge Isaac C. Parker (aka the Hanging Judge) and a 1920s drugstore with a working soda fountain. *320 Rogers Ave., (479) 783-7841, www. fortsmithmuseum.com.*

Hot Springs

Hot Springs National Park. The resort community of Hot Springs has been a national park since 1921. Several of the opulent bathhouses along Central Avenue (aka Bathhouse Row) have been restored, including the Fordyce, which contains a park visitors center and museum. To take the waters yourself, head to the Buckstaff—the only functioning bathhouse open within the national park—or the Quapaw Bath & Spa. *369 Central Ave., (501) 620-6715, www.nps.gov/hosp.*

The Gangster Museum of America. Ah, the good old bad old days, when gambling and booze were illegal—but that didn't stop anyone from enjoying them—and Hot Springs was a hot attraction for ne'er-do-wells. Al Capone vacationed here, enjoying the horse races, the spa, and his own room at the Arlington Hotel. He has his own exhibit at this museum, too. Memorabilia, photographs, and recorded accounts also highlight Owen "Owney" Madden, who's credited with putting Hot Springs on the gangster map, and Maxine Jones, once the city's richest madam. *510 Central Ave., (501) 318-1717, www.tgmoa.com.*

Fox Pass Pottery. This studio and shop, founded in 1973, features pieces by Jim and Barbara Larkin. He works at the potter's wheel, while she hand-builds her pieces. Although they're known for their unique glazes, the wood-fired salt kiln they use can create a pleasing finish without a traditionally applied glaze. *379 Fox Pass Cutoff, (501) 623-9906, foxpasspottery.com.*

Ozark National Forest

Thorncrown Chapel, Eureka Springs

Southern California's Coastal Playgrounds

Catalina Island

South of Los Angeles, the California coast is a veritable play land of natural and man-made attractions. This trip launches in Anaheim, home to Disney's first theme park, and continues south along the Pacific Coast Highway. It takes you through the breezy port of Long Beach and into ritzy surf towns like Huntington Beach.

Farther south, you'll motor through state parks, perhaps stopping at the mission in San Juan Capistrano (to uncover regional history) or Legoland (to find your inner child).

You'll end the drive in San Diego, a large, culturally rich beach city with fantastic weather all year, a buzzing Old Town, and one of the country's best zoos.

Atlas map J-7, p. 9

Distance: 139 miles point to point.

Type of Trip: Vacation Getaway; RV; Arts & Culture, Great Outdoors, History & Heritage, Picture Perfect.

Must Buy: Classic Mickey Mouse ears from the original Disney park; a souvenir beach towel from an oceanfront shop.

Must See: Disneyland, *Queen Mary*, Huntington Beach, Legoland, San Diego Zoo.

Worth Noting: California beaches are known for their sun, but fog and wind can make things chilly, even in summer. It's always best to have a sweatshirt, sweater, or windbreaker on hand.

Travel Tips: San Diego is known for sunny weather and bad traffic, especially on its crisscrossing freeways. Always add additional drive time.

In summer, beach regions get packed; reserve well in advance for hotels and campsites. Visit in fall for fantastic weather and a relatively empty coast.

Southern California's
Coastal Playgrounds

Anaheim

Disneyland. A true original, Disneyland's Magic Kingdom was the first theme park of its kind. It's truly geared towards kids of all ages, with staples like It's a Small World and Jungle Cruise for the whole family and more thrilling rides like Space Mountain and Matterhorn for older visitors. Then there are live performances, character breakfasts, princess makeovers, light shows like *Fantasmic* and *World of Color,* parades, and fireworks. *1313 S. Harbor Blvd., (714) 781-4000, disneyland. disney.go.com.*

Long Beach

Queen Mary. In service as an ocean liner from the 1930s to the '60s, the *Queen Mary* now sits in Long Beach harbor, attracting thousands of guests each year to its museum, restaurants, shops, and hotel rooms. Tour the historic cruise ship and a WW II troopship housed within its on-board museum while learning about the restoration project that helped land this vessel on the National Register of Historic Places. *1126 Queens Hwy., (877) 342-0738, www.queenmary.com.*

Catalina Island Ferry. Hop on an express ferry—you might see dolphins and whales in winter—to arrive at majestic Catalina Island in about an hour. Just 22 miles from the mainland, it seems worlds away with its bird sanctuaries, active bison population, and pristine beaches. (Reservations recommended.) *320 Golden Shore, (800) 481-3470, catalinaexpress.com.*

Huntington Beach

Huntington City Beach. This might just be southern California's most iconic beach. Known for its dependable surf, thin blonde sand, and miles of uninterrupted coastline, Huntington Beach hosts its share of surf and volleyball contests year round. Take a surf lesson from one of the instructors hanging out by the pier, shop for souvenirs at Kite Connection, or grab a cocktail on the patio of the Shorebreak Hotel. *Hwy. 1 and 2ⁿᵈ St., (714) 969-3492, www.surfcityusa.com.*

San Juan Capistrano

Mission San Juan Capistrano. Founded in 1775, this mission brought religious settlers to San Juan Capistrano. After almost a century of decay, Catholic conservationists refurbished the original Great Stone Church and acres of lush grounds. For a treat, explore the Serra Chapel, California's oldest operating church. You can picnic in the gardens, or join activities like fish feeding, basket weaving, gold panning, and crafting. *26801 Ortega Hwy., (949) 234-1300, www.missionsjc.com.*

San Clemente

San Clemente State Beach. Near the south end of San Clemente, this camping beach is popular with surfboarders and body surfers. There are a few notable surf breaks in the park, including a nice easy beach break right in front of the campground. More advanced surfers should walk about 15 minutes south of the parking area to Cottons, a local favorite. *225 Avenida Califia, (949) 492-3156, www.parks.ca.gov.*

Carlsbad

Legoland California Resort. More than 60 million Lego bricks are artfully arranged throughout both the park and the resort. You'll also find over 60 rides as well as water adventures, an aquarium, and Lego Minilands depicting everything from

Star Wars scenes to cities like Las Vegas. Weekend fireworks displays add to the dazzle. *One Legoland Dr., (760) 918-5346, california.legoland.com.*

San Diego

San Diego Air and Space Museum. This museum houses full-scale mock-ups of NASA spacecraft along with nearly 70 flying machines, including replicas of Wright gliders from 1901 and 1902. It's in Balboa Park, also home to the San Diego Museum of Art, the internationally acclaimed Old Globe Theater, a carousel, gardens, and trails. Pick up a Museum Pass for entry into multiple sites. *2001 Pan American Plaza, (619) 234-8291, www.sandiegoairandspace.org.*

San Diego Zoo. Considered by many to be the country's finest zoo, this spectacular 100-acre destination houses more than 3,700 animals from more than 650 species—including the largest collection of koalas outside of Australia and a Giant Panda from China. Note: The affiliated, 1,800-acre San Diego Zoo Safari Park is about 30 miles north. *2920 Zoo Dr., (619) 231-1515, zoo.sandiegozoo.org.*

Old Town San Diego State Historic Park. Stroll through California's first Spanish settlement, where original structures still stand and others have been restored. Costumed volunteers depict the history and culture and give cooking demonstrations. Most people stroll through the park and end up exploring the shops, restaurants, art galleries, and museums of nearby Old Town. *San Diego Ave. at Twiggs St., (619) 220-5422, www.parks.ca.gov.*

Torrey Pines State Natural Reserve & Beach. Oceanfront bluffs at this 2,000-acre reserve are dotted with wildflowers as well as fine examples of one of the rarest types of pine on the planet. Trails weave down to quiet beaches along sandstone shelves and offer peeks of gray whales migrating between Mexico and Alaska. *12600 N. Torrey Pines Rd., (858) 755-2063, torreypine.org.*

San Diego Zoo

Sunset in San Clemente

Tourism Contacts

On the road or before you go, log on to the official tourism website of your destination. These websites offer terrific ideas about organizing a visit and often include calendars of special events and activities. Prefer calling? Most states offer toll-free numbers.

United States

Alabama Tourism
(800) 252-2262
(334) 242-4169
www.alabama.travel

Alaska Tourism
(800) 862-5275
www.travelalaska.com

Arizona Office of Tourism
(866) 275-5816
(602) 364-3700
www.arizonaguide.com

Arkansas Parks & Tourism
(800) 628-8725
(501) 682-7777
www.arkansas.com

California Tourism
(877) 225-4367
(916) 444-4429
www.visitcalifornia.com

Colorado Tourism Office
(800) 265-6723
www.colorado.com

Connecticut Office of Tourism
(860) 256-2800
www.ctvisit.com

Delaware Tourism
(866) 284-7483
www.visitdelaware.com

Visit Florida
(888) 735-2872
(850) 488-5607
www.visitflorida.com

Visit Georgia
(800) 847-4842
www.exploregeorgia.org

Hawaii Visitors & Convention Bureau
(800) 464-2924
(808) 923-1811
www.gohawaii.com

Idaho Tourism
(800) 847-4843
(208) 334-2470
www.visitidaho.org

Illinois Office of Tourism
(800) 226-6632
www.enjoyillinois.com

Indiana Office of Tourism Development
(800) 677-9800
www.visitindiana.com

Iowa Tourism Office
(888) 472-6035
www.traveliowa.com

Kansas Department of Wildlife, Parks & Tourism
(800) 252-6727
(785) 296-2009
www.travelks.com

Kentucky Department of Travel & Tourism
(800) 225-8747
www.kentuckytourism.com

Louisiana Office of Tourism
(800) 994-8626
www.louisianatravel.com

Maine Office of Tourism
(888) 624-6345
www.visitmaine.com

Maryland Office of Tourism
(866) 639-3526
www.visitmaryland.org

Massachusetts Office of Travel & Tourism
(800) 227-6277
(617) 973-8500
www.massvacation.com

Travel Michigan
(888) 784-7328
www.michigan.org

Explore Minnesota Tourism
(888) 868-7476
(651) 296-5029
(651) 757-1845
www.exploreminnesota.com

Visit Mississippi
(866) 733-6477
(601) 359-3297
www.visitmississippi.org

Missouri Division of Tourism
(573) 751-4133
(800) 519-2100
www.visitmo.com

Montana Office of Tourism
(800) 847-4868
www.visitmt.com

Nebraska Tourism
(888) 444-1867
(877) 632-7275
www.visitnebraska.com

Nevada Commission on Tourism
(800) 638-2328
(775) 687-4322
www.travelnevada.com

New Hampshire Division of Travel and Tourism
(603) 271-2665
(800) 386-4664
www.visitnh.com

New Jersey Travel & Tourism
(609) 599-6540
www.visitnj.org

New Mexico Tourism Department
(505) 827-7336
www.newmexico.org

New York State Division of Tourism
(800) 225-5697
www.iloveny.com

North Carolina Travel & Tourism
(800) 847-4862
www.visitnc.com

North Dakota Tourism
(800) 435-5663
(701) 328-2525
www.ndtourism.com

Tourism Ohio
(800) 282-5393
www.discoverohio.com

Oklahoma Tourism & Recreation Department
(800) 652-6552
www.travelok.com

Travel Oregon
(800) 547-7842
www.traveloregon.com

Pennsylvania Tourism Office
(800) 847-4872
www.visitpa.com

Rhode Island Tourism Division
(401) 278-9100
(800) 556-2484
www.visitrhodeisland.com

South Carolina Department of Parks, Recreation & Tourism
(803) 734-1700
www.discoversouthcarolina.com

South Dakota Department of Tourism
(800) 732-5682
www.travelsouthdakota.com

Tennessee Department of Tourist Development
(615) 741-2159
www.tnvacation.com

Texas Tourism
(800) 452-9292
www.traveltex.com

Utah Office of Tourism
(800) 200-1160
(801) 538-1900
www.visitutah.com

Vermont Department of Tourism and Marketing
(800) 837-6668
(800) 882-4386
www.vermontvacation.com

Virginia Tourism
(800) 847-4882
www.virginia.org

Washington Tourism
(800) 544-1800
www.experiencewa.com

Destination DC
(800) 422-8644
(202) 789-7000
www.washington.org

West Virginia Division of Tourism
(800) 225-5982
(304) 558-2200
www.wvtourism.com
gotowv.com

Wisconsin Department of Tourism
(800) 432-8747
(608) 266-2161
www.travelwisconsin.com

Wyoming Office of Tourism
(800) 225-5996
(307) 777-7777
www.wyomingtourism.org

Canada

Travel Alberta
(800) 252-3782
www.travelalberta.us

Destination British Columbia
(604) 660-2861
www.hellobc.com

Travel Manitoba
(800) 665-0040
(204) 927-7838
www.travelmanitoba.com

Tourism New Brunswick
(800) 561-0123
www.tourismnewbrunswick.ca

Newfoundland & Labrador Tourism
(800) 563-6353
(709) 729-2830
www.newfoundlandlabrador.com

Northwest Territories Tourism
(800) 661-0788
www.spectacularnwt.com

Nova Scotia Tourism Agency
(800) 565-0000
(902) 424-5000
www.novascotia.com

Ontario Travel
(800) 668-2746
www.ontariotravel.net

Prince Edward Island Tourism
(800) 463-4734
www.tourismpei.com

Tourisme Québec
(877) 266-5687
(514) 873-2015
www.bonjourquebec.com

Tourism Saskatchewan
(877) 237-2273
(306) 787-2300
www.tourismsaskatchewan.com

Tourism Yukon
(800) 661-0494
www.travelyukon.com

Mexico

Mexico Tourism Board
(800) 446-3942
www.visitmexico.com/en

Puerto Rico

Tourism Company of Puerto Rico
(800) 866-7827
www.puertorico.com

Road Work

Road construction and road conditions resources

Road closed. Single lane traffic ahead. Detour.
When you are on the road, knowledge is power. Let Rand McNally help you avoid situations that can result in delays, or worse. Use the state and province websites and hotlines listed on this page for road construction and road conditions information.

United States

Alabama
(888) 588-2848
www.dot.state.al.us

Alaska
511
511.alaska.gov
www.dot.state.ak.us

Arizona
511
(888) 411-7623
www.az511.com
www.azdot.gov

Arkansas
(800) 245-1672
(501) 569-2374
(501) 569-2000
www.arkansashighways.com

California
(800) 427-7623
www.dot.ca.gov
Los Angeles/metro area:
511, www.go511.com
Sacramento Region:
511, www.sacregion511.org
San Diego area:
511, www.511sd.com
San Francisco Bay area:
511, www.511.org

Colorado
511
(303) 639-1111
(303) 573-7623
www.cotrip.org

Connecticut
(860) 594-2000
(860) 594-2650
www.ct.gov/dot

Delaware
(800) 652-5600
(302) 760-2080
www.deldot.gov

Florida
511
(866) 374-3368
www.fl511.com
www.dot.state.fl.us

Georgia
511
(888) 635-8287
(877) 694-2511
(404) 635-8000
www.511ga.org

Hawaii
(808) 587-2220
hidot/hawaii.gov

Idaho
511
(888) 432-7623
www.511.idaho.gov
www.itd.idaho.gov

Illinois
(800) 452-4368
(312) 368-4636
www.gettingaroundillinois.com
www.dot.il.gov

Indiana
(866) 849-1368
(317) 232-5533
www.in.gov/dot

Iowa
511
(800) 288-1047
www.511ia.org
www.iowadot.gov

Kansas
511
(866) 511-5368
(785) 296-3566
511.ksdot.org
www.ksdot.org

Kentucky
511
(866) 737-3767
www.511.ky.gov
transportation.ky.gov/

Louisiana
511
(877) 452-3683
www.511la.org
www.dotd.la.gov

Maine
511
(866) 282-7578
(207) 624-3595
www.511maine.gov
www.maine.gov/mdot

Maryland
511
(800) 323-6742
(410) 582-5650
In Maryland: (800) 543-2515
www.md511.org
www.roads.maryland.gov

Massachusetts
511
Metro Boston: (617) 986-5511
Central: (508) 499-5511
Western: (413) 754-5511
www.mass511.com
www.mhd.state.ma.us

Michigan
(800) 381-8477
(517) 335-3084
www.michigan.gov/drive

Get the Info from the 511 hotline

The U.S. Federal Highway Administration has begun implementing a national system of highway and road conditions/construction information for travelers. Under the new plan, travelers can dial 511 and get up-to-date information on roads and highways.

Implementation of 511 is the responsibility of state and local agencies.

For more details, visit: www.fhwa.dot.gov/trafficinfo/511.htm.

Minnesota
511
In MN (800) 657-3774
(651) 296-3000
www.511mn.org
www.dot.state.mn.us

Mississippi
511
(601) 987-1211
(601) 359-7001
www.mdot.ms.gov
www.mdottraffic.com

Missouri
(888) 275-6636
(573) 751-2551
www.modot.org

Montana
511
(800) 226-7623
(406) 444-6200
www.mdt511.com
www.mdt.mt.gov

Nebraska
511
(800) 906-9069
www.511.nebraska.gov
www.dor.state.ne.us

Nevada
511
(877) 687-6237
(775) 888-7000
www.nevadadot.com
www.nvroads.com

New Hampshire
511
(603) 271-6862
www.nhtmc.com
www.nh.gov/dot

New Jersey
511
(866) 511-6538
www.511nj.org
www.state.nj.us/transportation

New Mexico
511
(800) 432-4269
(505) 827-5100
www.nmroads.com
www.dot.state.nm.us

New York
511
(888) 465-1169
www.511ny.org
www.dot.ny.gov
Thruway:
(800) 847-8929
www.thruway.ny.gov

North Carolina
511
(877) 511-4662
www.ncdot.gov
www.ncdot.gov/travel/511

North Dakota
511
(866) 696-3511
(855) 637-6237
www.dot.nd.gov
www.dot.nd.gov/travel-info-v2/

Ohio
(614) 466-7170
www.dot.state.oh.us
www.buckeyetraffic.org
Cincinnati/metro area:
511
Ohio Turnpike:
(440) 234-2030
(440) 234-2081
www.ohioturnpike.org

Oklahoma
(844) 465-4997
www.okladot.state.ok.us
okroads.org

Oregon
511
(800) 977-6368
(503) 588-2941
www.oregon.gov/odot
www.tripcheck.com

Pennsylvania
511
(888) 783-6783
www.dot.state.pa.us

Rhode Island
511
(888) 401-4511
(401) 222-2450
www.dot.ri.gov/travel

South Carolina
511
(877) 511-4672
(855) 467-2368
www.dot.state.sc.us
www.511sc.org/

South Dakota
511
(866) 697-3511
www.sddot.com
safetravelusa.com/sd/

Tennessee
511
(877) 244-0065
www.tn511.com
www.tdot.state.tn.us

Texas
(800) 452-9292
(512) 463-8588
www.txdot.gov
www.drivetexas.org

Utah
511
(866) 511-8824
(801) 887-3700
www.udot.utah.gov
www.utahcommuterlink.com

Vermont
511
www.511vt.com
www.aot.state.vt.us

Virginia
511
(800) 578-4111
(800) 367-7623
www.511virginia.org
www.virginiadot.org/travel

Washington
511
(800) 695-7623
www.wsdot.wa.gov/traffic

Washington, D.C.
311
(202) 737-4404
(202) 673-6813
ddot.dc.gov

West Virginia
511
(877) 982-7623
www.wv511.org
www.transportation.wv.gov

Wisconsin
511
(866) 511-9472
www.511wi.gov

Wyoming
511
(888) 996-7623
www.wyoroad.info

Canada

Alberta
(877) 262-4997
www.ama.ab.ca

British Columbia
(800) 550-4997
www.drivebc.ca

Manitoba
511
(877) 627-6237
(204) 945-3704
www.manitoba.ca/roadinfo
www.manitoba.ca

New Brunswick
511
(888) 747-7006
(506) 453-3939
(800) 561-4063
www.gnb.ca/roads

Newfoundland & Labrador
Avalon Region (709) 729-2382
Eastern Region (709) 466-4120
Central Region (709) 292-4300
Western Region (709) 635-4127
Labrador Region (709) 896-7840
www.roads.gov.nl.ca

Nova Scotia
511
(902) 424-3933
In Canada, outside NS:
(888) 780-4440
511.gov.ns.ca/map

Ontario
511
(800) 268-4686
In Toronto: (416) 235-4686
www.mto.gov.on.ca/english/
traveller/

Prince Edward Island
511
(902) 368-4770
In Canada: (855) 241-2680
www.gov.pe.ca/roadconditions

Québec
511
(888) 355-0511
In Québec: (877) 393-2363
www.quebec511.gouv.qc.ca/en/

Saskatchewan
In Saskatchewan only:
(888) 335-7623
Saskatoon area: (306) 933-8333
Regina area: (306) 787-7623
www.highways.gov.sk.ca/
road-conditions

Mexico

www.sct.gob.mx/carreteras

Puerto Rico

www.dtop.gov.pr/carretera

© Rand McNally

National Monuments and Memorials

1M Agate Fossil Beds	E-6
2M Alibates Flint Quarries	G-6
3M Admiralty Island	J-2
4M Agua Fria	G-3
5M Aniakchak	J-1
6M Aztec Ruins	F-5
7M Basin and Range	E-3
8M Berryessa Snow Mountain	D-1
9M Browns Canyon	F-5
10M Cabrillo	G-2
11M Canyon de Chelly	F-4
12M Cape Krusenstern	I-1
13M Capulin Volcano	F-6
14M Casa Grande Ruins	G-3
15M Castillo de San Marcos	H-12
16M Cedar Breaks	F-4
17M Chiricahua	H-4
18M Colorado	E-5
19M Craters of the Moon	D-4
20M Devils Tower	D-6
21M Dinosaur	E-5
22M Effigy Mounds	G-5
23M El Malpais	G-5
24M El Morro	G-4
25M Florissant Fossil Beds	E-5
26M Fort Clatsop	B-2
27M Fort Frederica	H-12
28M Fort Matanzas	H-12
29M Fort Monroe	F-13
30M Fort Ord	E-1
31M Fort Pulaski	H-12
32M Fort Sumter	G-12
33M Fort Union	G-5
34M Fossil Butte	D-4
35M George Washington Carver	F-8
36M Giant Sequoia	F-2
37M Gila Cliff Dwellings	G-4
38M Grand Canyon-Parashant	F-3
39M Grand Portage	C-9
40M Grand Staircase-Escalante	F-4
41M Hagerman Fossil Beds	D-3
42M Homestead	E-6
43M Hovenweep	F-4
44M Jewel Cave	D-6
45M Lava Beds	D-2
46M Montezuma Castle	G-4
47M Mount Rushmore	D-6
48M Mount St. Helens	B-2
49M Natural Bridges	F-4
50M Navajo	F-4
51M Newberry Volcanic	C-2
52M Ocmulgee	G-11
53M Organ Mountains Desert Peaks	H-5
54M Organ Pipe Cactus	G-3
55M Petroglyph	G-5
56M Pipe Spring	F-3
57M Pipestone	D-8
58M Rainbow Bridge	F-4
59M Rio Grande del Norte	F-5
60M Russell Cave	G-11
61M Salinas Pueblo Missions	G-5
62M San Gabriel Mountains	F-2
63M Scotts Bluff	E-6
64M Sonoran Desert	G-3
65M Sunset Crater Volcano	F-4
66M Timpanogos Cave	E-4
67M Tonto	G-4
68M Tuzigoot	G-3
69M Upper Missouri River Breaks	B-5
70M Vermilion Cliffs	F-4
71M White Sands	H-5
72M Wright Brothers	F-13
73M Wupatki	F-4

National Parks

1P Acadia	C-14	20P Glacier Bay	J-2
2P Arches	E-4	21P Glacier	B-4
3P Badlands	D-6	22P Grand Canyon	F-3
4P Big Bend	I-6	23P Grand Teton	D-4
5P Biscayne	J-13	24P Great Basin	E-3
6P Black Canyon	F-5	25P Great Sand Dunes	F-5
7P Bryce Canyon	F-4	26P Great Smoky Mtns.	G-11
8P Canyonlands	F-4	27P Guadalupe Mtns.	H-5
9P Capitol Reef	E-4	28P Haleakalá	I-4
10P Carlsbad Caverns	H-5	29P Hawai'i Volcanoes	I-5
11P Channel Islands	F-1	30P Hot Springs	G-9
12P Congaree	G-12	31P Isle Royale	C-9
13P Crater Lake	C-2	32P Joshua Tree	G-2
14P Cuyahoga Valley	E-11	33P Katmai	J-1
15P Death Valley	F-2	34P Kenai Fjords	J-1
16P Denali	I-1	35P Kings Canyon	F-2
17P Dry Tortugas	J-12	36P Kobuk Valley	I-1
18P Everglades	J-13	37P Lake Clark	J-1
19P Gates of the Arctic	I-1	38P Lassen Volcanic	D-2
		39P Mammoth Cave	F-10
40P Mesa Verde	F-5		
41P Mt. Rainier	B-2		
42P North Cascades	B-3		
43P Olympic	B-2		
44P Petrified Forest	G-4		
45P Pinnacles	E-1		
46P Redwood	C-1		
47P Rocky Mountain	E-5		
48P Saguaro	H-4		
49P Sequoia	F-2		
50P Shenandoah	E-12		
51P Theodore Roosevelt	C-6		
52P Voyageurs	C-8		
53P Wind Cave	D-6		
54P Wrangell-St. Elias	I-2		
55P Yellowstone	C-5		
56P Yosemite	E-2		
57P Zion	F-3		

Alabama

Population: 4,779,736
Land Area: 50,645 sq. mi.
Capital: Montgomery

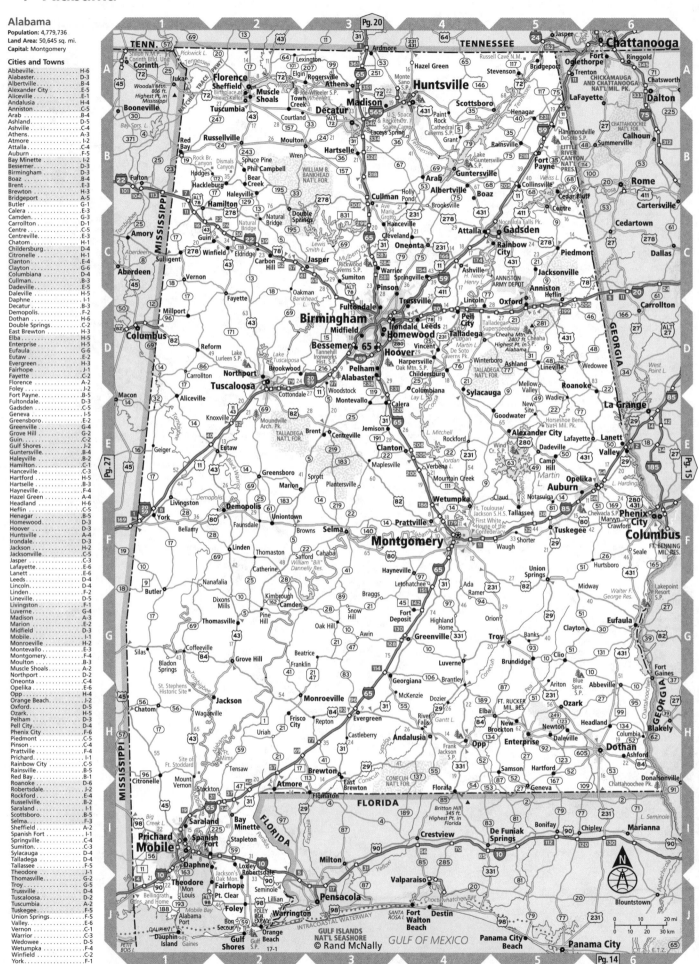

© Rand McNally

NOTE: Maps are not always in alphabetical order.
See Page 1 for map location in this atlas.

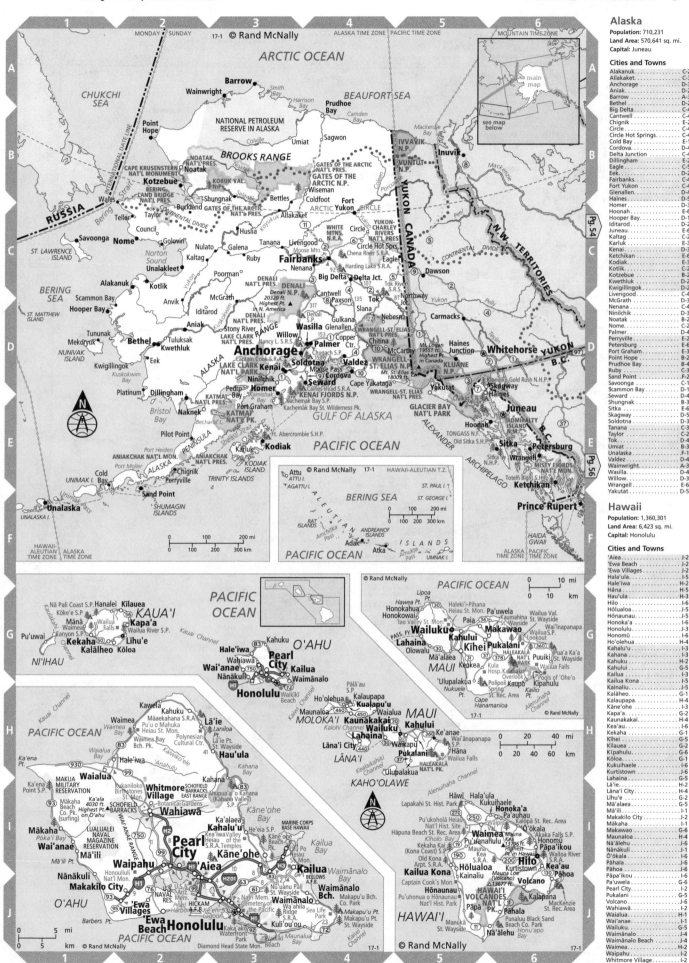

Alaska

Population: 710,231
Land Area: 570,641 sq. mi.
Capital: Juneau

Cities and Towns

Hawaii

Population: 1,360,301
Land Area: 6,423 sq. mi.
Capital: Honolulu

Cities and Towns

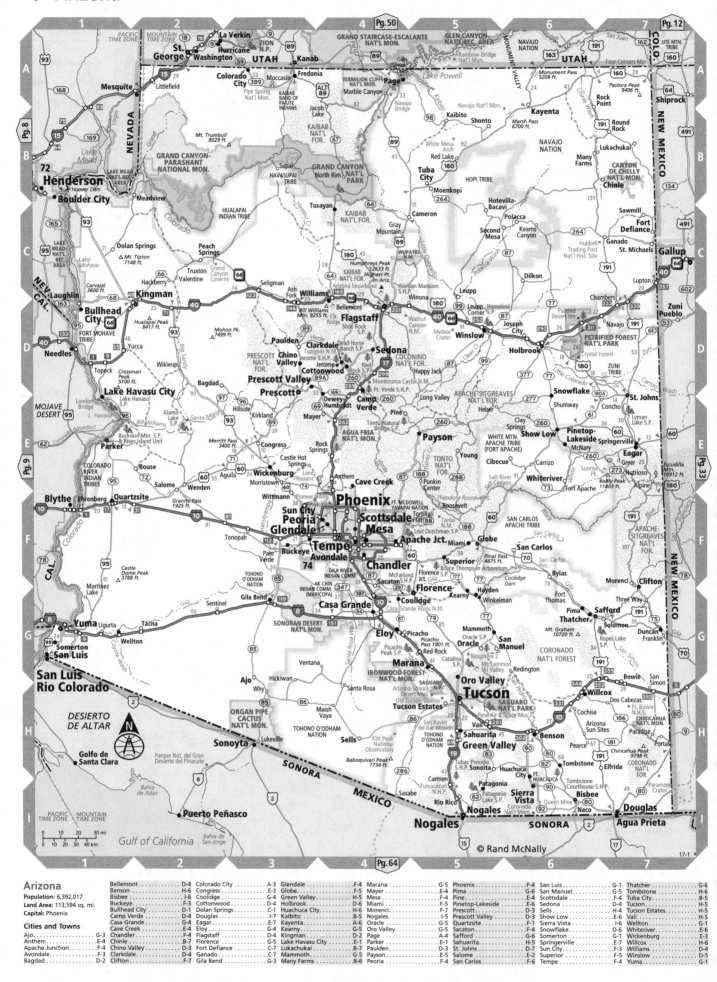

NOTE: Maps are not always in alphabetical order.
See Page 1 for map location in this atlas.

Arkansas   7

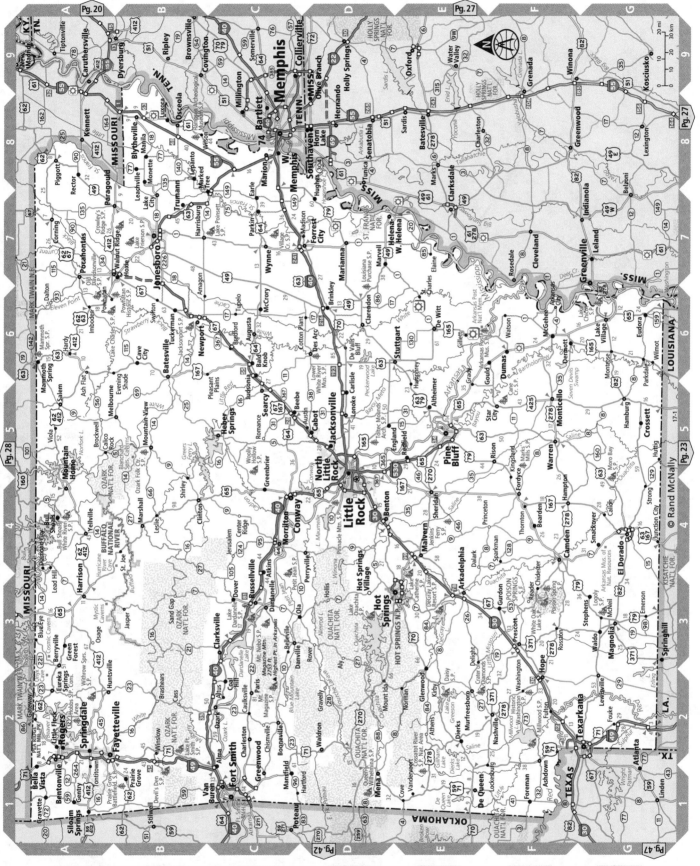

© Rand McNally

Arkansas

Population: 2,915,918
Land Area: 52,035 sq. mi.
Capital: Little Rock

Cities and Towns

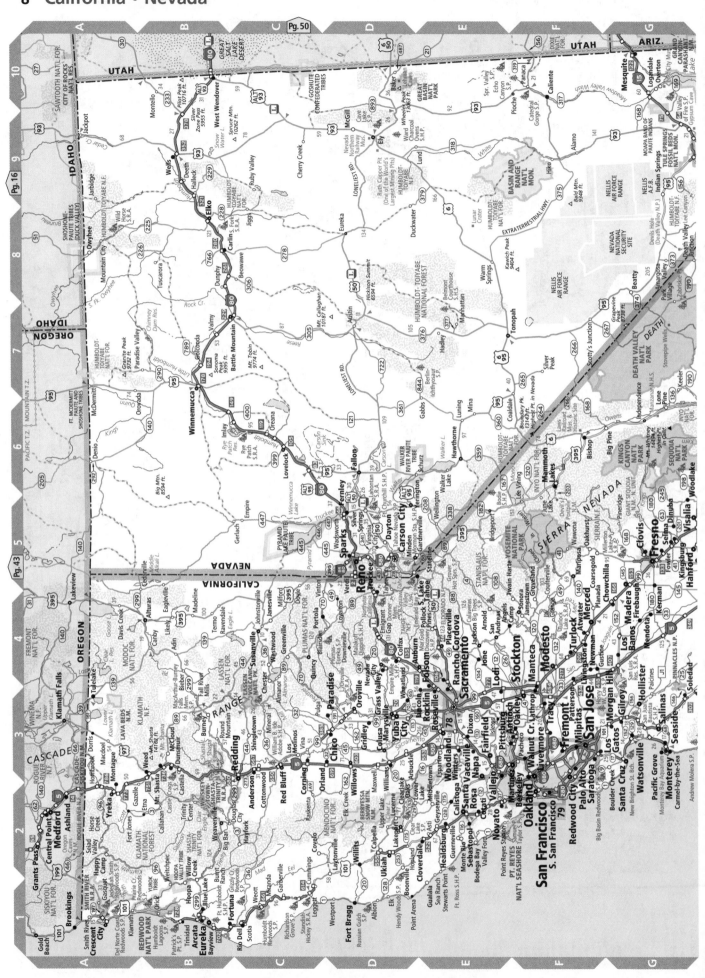

NOTE: Maps are not always in alphabetical order.
See Page 1 for map location in this atlas.

California • Nevada 9

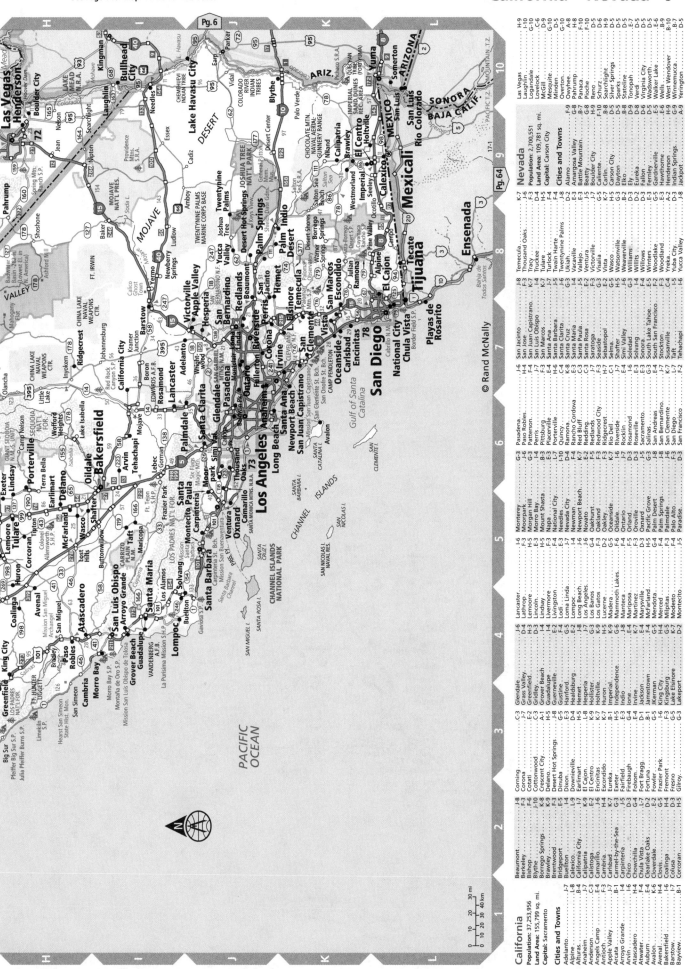

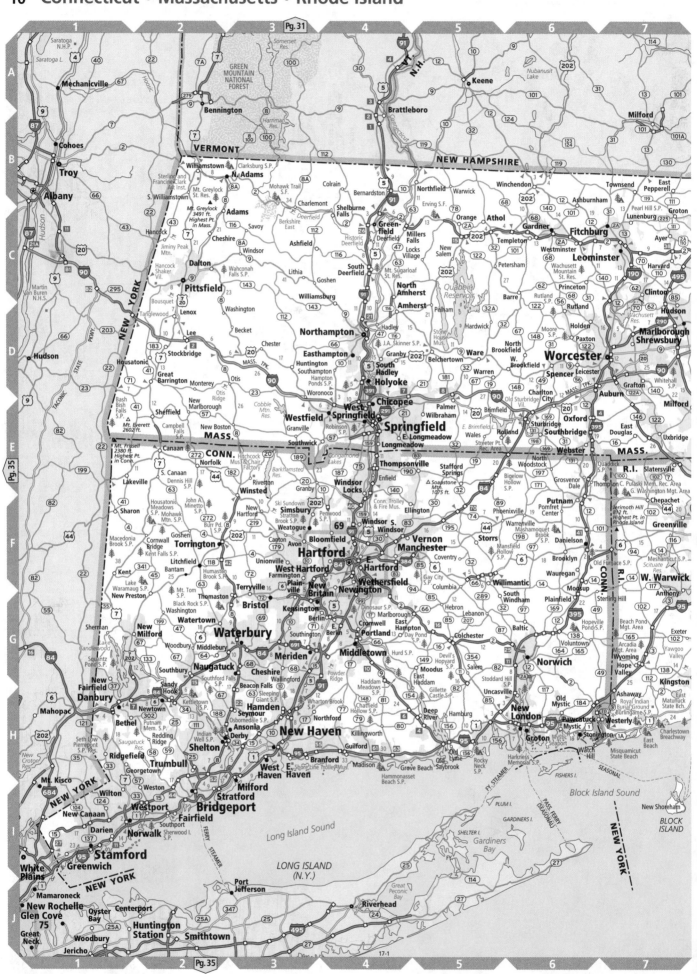

NOTE: Maps are not always in alphabetical order.
See Page 1 for map location in this atlas.

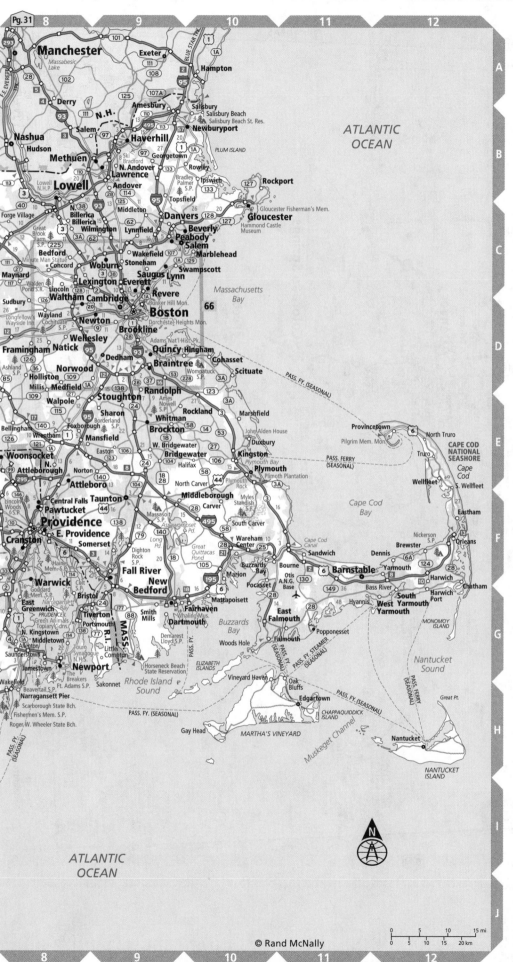

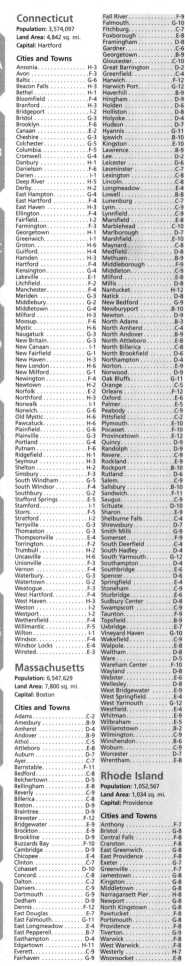

Connecticut

Population: 3,574,097
Land Area: 4,842 sq. mi.
Capital: Hartford

Cities and Towns

Ansonia H-3
Avon F-3
Baltic G-6
Beacon Falls H-3
Bethel H-1
Bloomfield F-4
Branford H-3
Bridgeport I-2
Bristol G-3
Brooklyn F-6
Canaan E-2
Cheshire G-3
Colchester G-5
Columbia F-5
Cromwell G-4
Danbury H-1
Danielson F-6
Darien I-1
Deep River H-5
Derby H-2
East Hampton G-4
East Hartford F-4
East Haven H-3
Ellington F-4
Fairfield I-2
Farmington G-3
Georgetown H-1
Greenwich I-1
Groton H-6
Guilford H-4
Hamden H-3
Hartford G-4
Kensington G-4
Lakeville E-1
Litchfield F-2
Manchester F-4
Meriden G-3
Middlebury G-2
Middletown G-4
Milford H-3
Moosup F-6
Mystic H-6
Naugatuck H-2
New Britain G-3
New Canaan I-1
New Fairfield G-1
New Haven H-3
New London H-6
New Milford G-1
Newington G-4
Newtown H-2
Norfolk E-2
Northford H-3
Norwalk I-1
Norwich G-6
Old Mystic H-6
Pawcatuck H-6
Plainfield G-6
Plainville G-3
Portland G-4
Putnam F-6
Ridgefield H-1
Seymour H-3
Shelton H-2
Simsbury F-3
South Windham G-5
South Windsor F-4
Southbury G-2
Stafford Springs E-5
Stamford I-1
Storrs F-5
Stratford I-2
Terryville G-3
Thomaston G-3
Thompsonville E-4
Torrington F-2
Trumbull H-2
Uncasville H-6
Unionville F-3
Vernon F-4
Waterbury G-3
Waterford G-2
Weatogue F-3
West Hartford F-4
West Haven H-3
Weston I-2
Westport I-2
Wethersfield F-4
Willimantic F-5
Wilton I-1
Windsor F-4
Windsor Locks E-4
Winsted E-3

Massachusetts

Population: 6,547,629
Land Area: 7,800 sq. mi.
Capital: Boston

Cities and Towns

Adams C-2
Amesbury B-9
Amherst C-4
Andover B-9
Athol C-5
Attleboro E-8
Auburn D-7
Ayer C-7
Barnstable F-11
Bedford C-8
Belchertown D-5
Bellingham E-8
Beverly C-9
Billerica C-8
Boston D-9
Braintree D-9
Brewster F-12
Bridgewater E-9
Brockton E-9
Brookline D-9
Buzzards Bay F-10
Cambridge D-9
Chicopee D-4
Clinton C-7
Cohasset D-10
Concord C-8
Dalton C-2
Danvers C-9
Dartmouth F-9
Dedham D-9
Dennis F-12
East Douglas E-7
East Falmouth G-11
East Longmeadow . . . E-4
East Pepperell B-7
Easthampton D-4
Edgartown H-11
Everett C-9
Fairhaven G-9

Fall River F-9
Falmouth G-10
Fitchburg C-7
Foxborough E-8
Framingham D-8
Gardner C-6
Georgetown B-9
Gloucester C-10
Great Barrington D-2
Greenfield C-4
Harwich F-12
Harwich Port G-12
Haverhill B-9
Hingham D-9
Holden D-6
Holliston D-8
Holyoke D-4
Hudson D-7
Hyannis G-11
Ipswich B-10
Kingston E-10
Lawrence B-9
Lee D-2
Leicester D-6
Leominster C-7
Lexington C-8
Lincoln C-8
Longmeadow E-4
Lowell B-8
Lunenburg C-7
Lynn C-9
Lynnfield C-9
Mansfield E-8
Marblehead C-10
Marlborough D-7
Marshfield E-10
Maynard C-8
Medfield D-8
Methuen B-9
Middleborough E-9
Middleton C-9
Milford D-8
Millis D-8
Nantucket H-12
Natick D-8
New Bedford G-9
Newburyport B-10
Newton D-9
North Adams B-3
North Amherst C-4
North Andover B-9
North Attleboro E-8
North Billerica C-8
North Brookfield D-6
Northampton D-4
Norton E-8
Norwood D-9
Oak Bluffs G-11
Orange C-5
Orleans F-12
Oxford E-6
Palmer E-5
Peabody C-9
Pittsfield C-2
Plymouth E-10
Pocasset F-10
Provincetown E-12
Quincy D-9
Randolph D-9
Revere C-9
Rockland D-9
Rockport B-10
Rutland D-6
Salem C-9
Salisbury B-10
Sandwich F-11
Saugus C-9
Scituate D-10
Sharon E-9
Shelburne Falls C-4
Shrewsbury D-7
Smith Mills G-9
Somerset F-9
South Deerfield C-4
South Hadley D-4
South Yarmouth G-12
Southampton D-4
Southbridge E-6
Spencer D-6
Springfield E-4
Stoneham C-9
Sturbridge E-6
Sudbury Center D-8
Swampscott C-9
Taunton F-9
Topsfield B-9
Uxbridge E-7
Vineyard Haven G-10
Wakefield C-9
Walpole D-8
Waltham D-8
Ware D-5
Wareham Center F-10
Wayland D-8
Webster E-6
Wellesley D-8
West Bridgewater . . . E-9
West Springfield E-4
West Yarmouth G-12
Westfield E-4
Whitman E-9
Wilbraham E-5
Williamstown B-2
Wilmington C-9
Winchendon B-6
Woburn C-9
Worcester D-7
Wrentham E-8

Rhode Island

Population: 1,052,567
Land Area: 1,034 sq. mi.
Capital: Providence

Cities and Towns

Anthony F-7
Bristol G-8
Central Falls F-8
Cranston F-8
East Greenwich G-8
East Providence F-8
Exeter G-7
Greenville F-7
Jamestown G-8
Kingston G-8
Middletown G-8
Narragansett Pier H-8
Newport G-8
North Kingstown G-8
Pawtucket F-8
Portsmouth G-8
Providence F-8
Tiverton G-8
Warwick F-8
West Warwick F-8
Westerly H-7
Woonsocket E-8

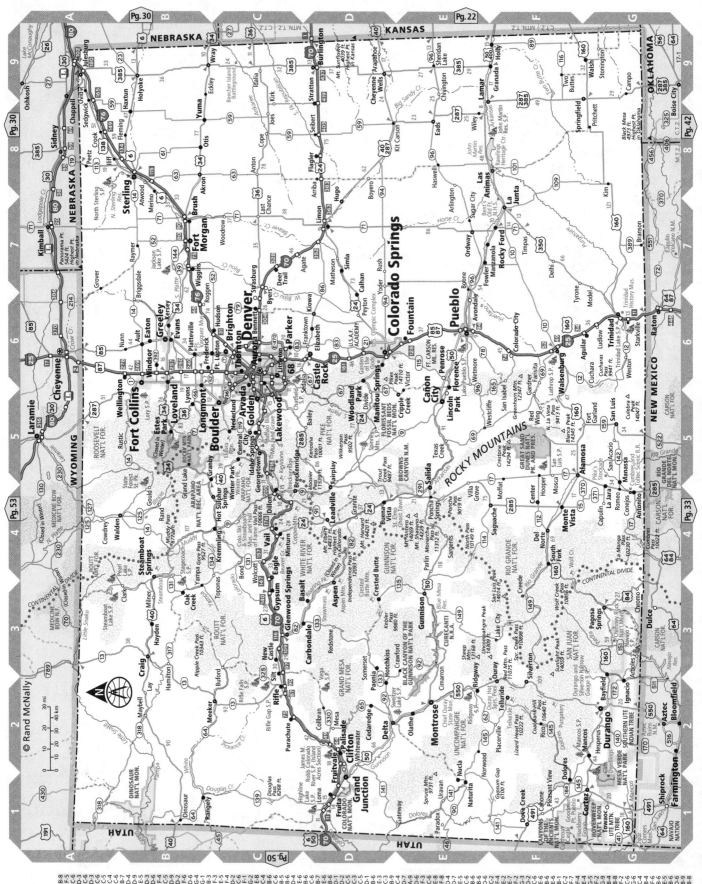

NOTE: Maps are not always in alphabetical order. See Page 1 for map location in this atlas.

Delaware • Maryland 13

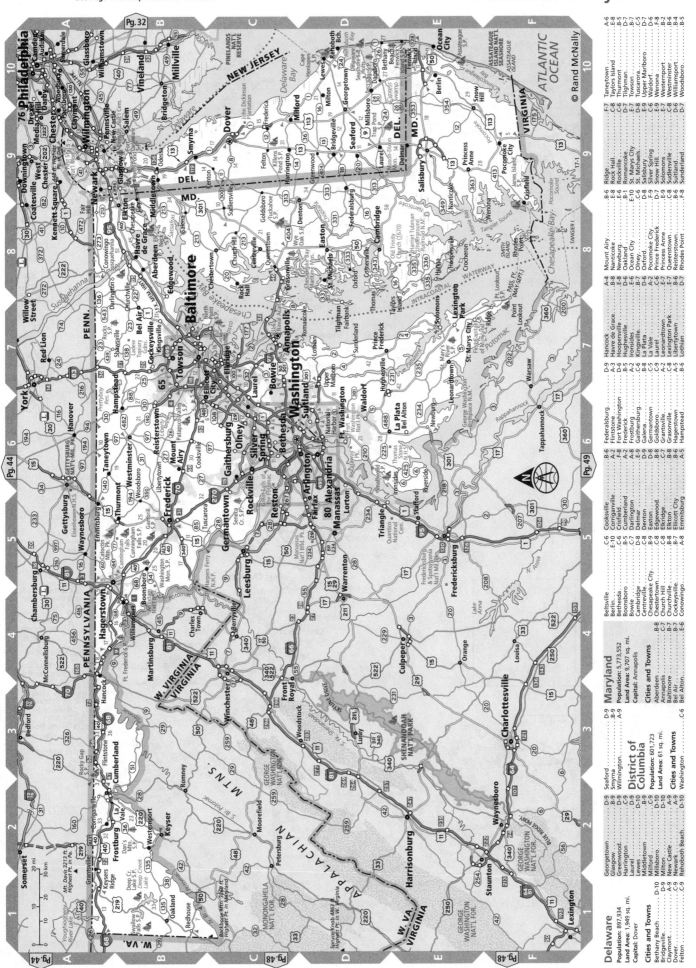

© Rand McNally

ATLANTIC OCEAN

Pg. 32 · Pg. 44 · Pg. 49 · Pg. 48

Florida

Population: 18,801,310
Land Area: 53,625 sq. mi.
Capital: Tallahassee

GEORGIA

ATLANTIC OCEAN

GULF OF MEXICO

Jacksonville

Tallahassee

Orlando

Tampa

St. Petersburg

Fort Lauderdale

Miami

Key West

© Rand McNally

NOTE: Maps are not always in alphabetical order.
See Page 1 for map location in this atlas.

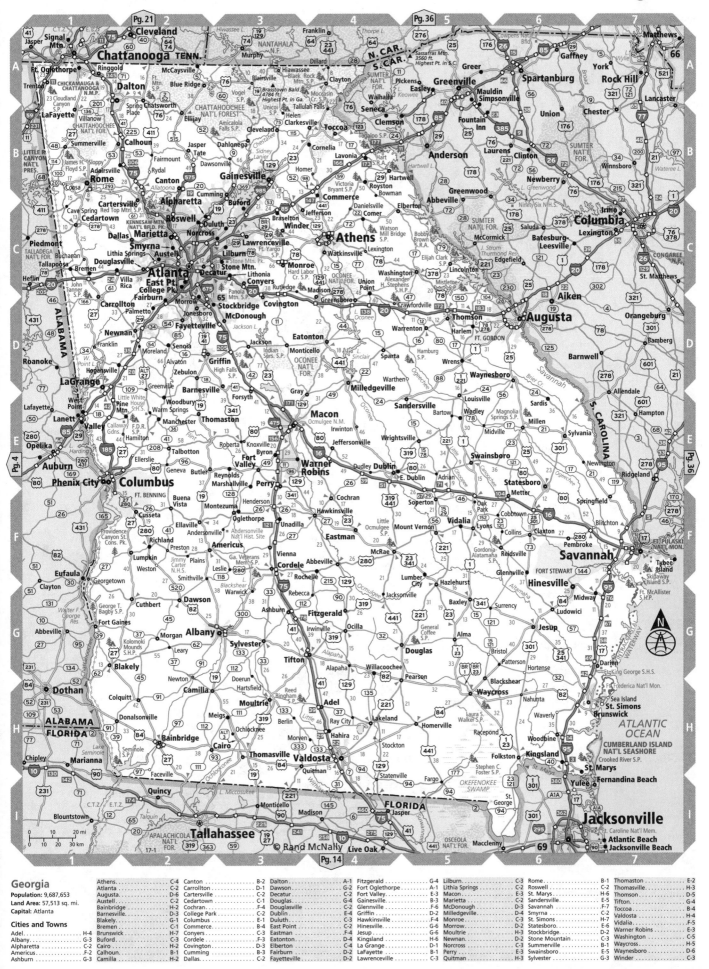

© Rand McNally

Georgia

Population: 9,687,653
Land Area: 57,513 sq. mi.
Capital: Atlanta

Cities and Towns

Idaho

Population: 1,567,582
Land Area: 82,643 sq. mi.
Capital: Boise

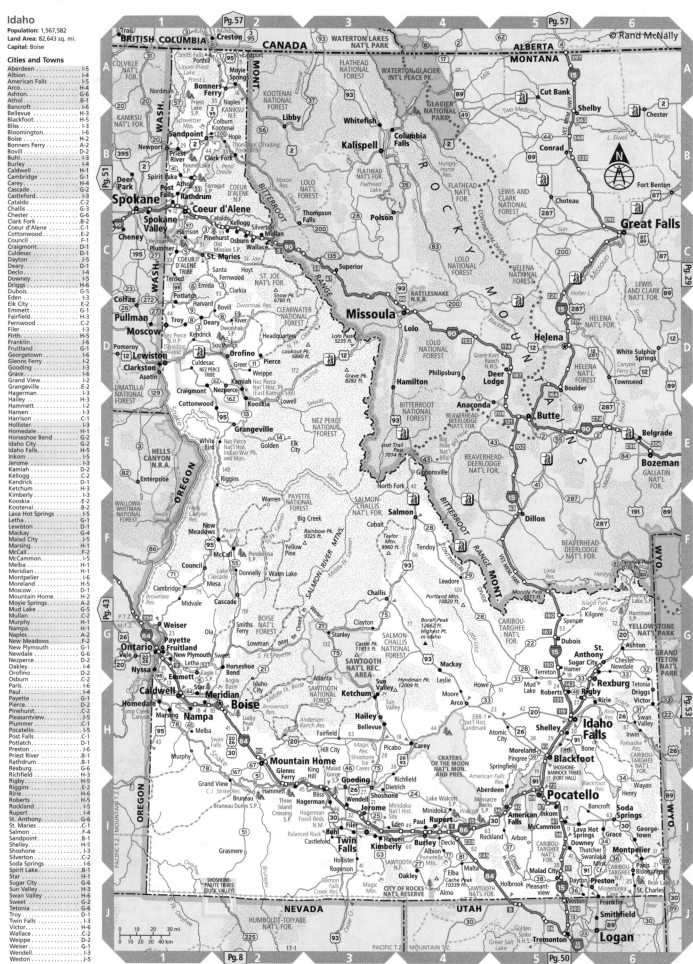

© Rand McNally

NOTE: Maps are not always in alphabetical order.
See Page 1 for map location in this atlas.

Illinois
Population: 12,830,632
Land Area: 55,519 sq. mi.
Capital: Springfield

Cities and Towns

Albion	H-5
Aledo	C-2
Alton	G-2
Arlington Heights	B-5
Aurora	B-5
Belleville	H-3
Belvidere	A-4
Benton	I-4
Bloomington	D-4
Cairo	J-4
Cambridge	C-3
Canton	D-3
Carbondale	I-4
Carlinville	F-3
Carlyle	G-4
Carmi	H-5
Carrollton	F-2
Carthage	D-1
Centralia	H-4
Champaign	E-5
Charleston	F-5
Chester	I-3
Chicago	B-6
Chicago Heights	C-6
Clinton	E-4
Collinsville	G-3
Crete	C-6
Crystal Lake	A-5
Danville	E-6
Decatur	E-4
DeKalb	B-5
Des Plaines	B-5
Dixon	B-3
East Moline	C-2
East St. Louis	G-3
Edwardsville	G-3
Effingham	G-5
Elgin	B-5
Eureka	D-4
Evanston	B-6
Fairfield	H-5
Forsyth	E-4
Freeport	A-3
Galena	A-2
Galesburg	C-3
Granite City	G-3
Greenville	G-3
Harrisburg	I-5
Havana	E-3
Herrin	I-4
Highland Park	A-6
Hillsboro	G-3
Jacksonville	F-2
Jerseyville	F-2
Joliet	B-5
Jonesboro	I-3
Kankakee	C-5
Kewanee	C-4
La Salle	C-4
Lacon	C-3
Lake Forest	A-5
Lawrenceville	G-6
Lewistown	D-3
Libertyville	A-5
Lincoln	E-4
Lisle	B-5
Louisville	G-5
Macomb	D-2
Manteno	C-6
Marion	I-4
Marshall	F-6
Mattoon	F-5
McHenry	A-5
McLeansboro	H-5
Metropolis	J-4
Moline	C-2
Monmouth	D-2
Monticello	E-5
Morris	C-5
Morrison	B-3
Morton	D-3
Mount Carmel	H-6
Mount Carroll	B-3
Mount Sterling	E-2
Mount Vernon	H-4
Murphysboro	I-4
Naperville	B-5
Nashville	H-4
New Lenox	C-5
Newton	G-5
Normal	D-4
O'Fallon	G-3
Olney	G-5
Oquawka	C-2
Oregon	B-4
Oswego	B-5
Ottawa	C-4
Paris	F-6
Paxton	D-5
Pekin	D-3
Peoria	D-3
Peru	C-4
Petersburg	E-3
Pinckneyville	H-4
Pittsfield	F-2
Plainfield	B-5
Pontiac	D-4
Princeton	C-3
Quincy	E-1
Rantoul	E-5
Robinson	G-6
Rock Falls	B-3
Rock Island	C-2
Rockford	A-4
Rushville	D-2
St. Charles	B-5
Salem	G-4
Shawneetown	I-5
Shelbyville	F-4
Shorewood	C-5
Skokie	B-6
Springfield	E-3
Sterling	B-3
Streator	C-4
Sycamore	B-4
Taylorville	F-4
Toulon	C-3
Tuscola	E-5
Urbana	E-5
Vandalia	G-4
Virginia	E-2
Washington	D-3
Waterloo	H-2
Watseka	D-6
Waukegan	A-5
Wheaton	B-5
Wilmette	B-6
Winchester	F-2
Winnetka	B-6
Woodstock	A-5
Zion	A-6

© Rand McNally

Indiana

Population: 6,483,802
Land Area: 35,826 sq. mi.
Capital: Indianapolis

© Rand McNally

NOTE: Maps are not always in alphabetical order.
See Page 1 for map location in this atlas.

Iowa 19

© Rand McNally

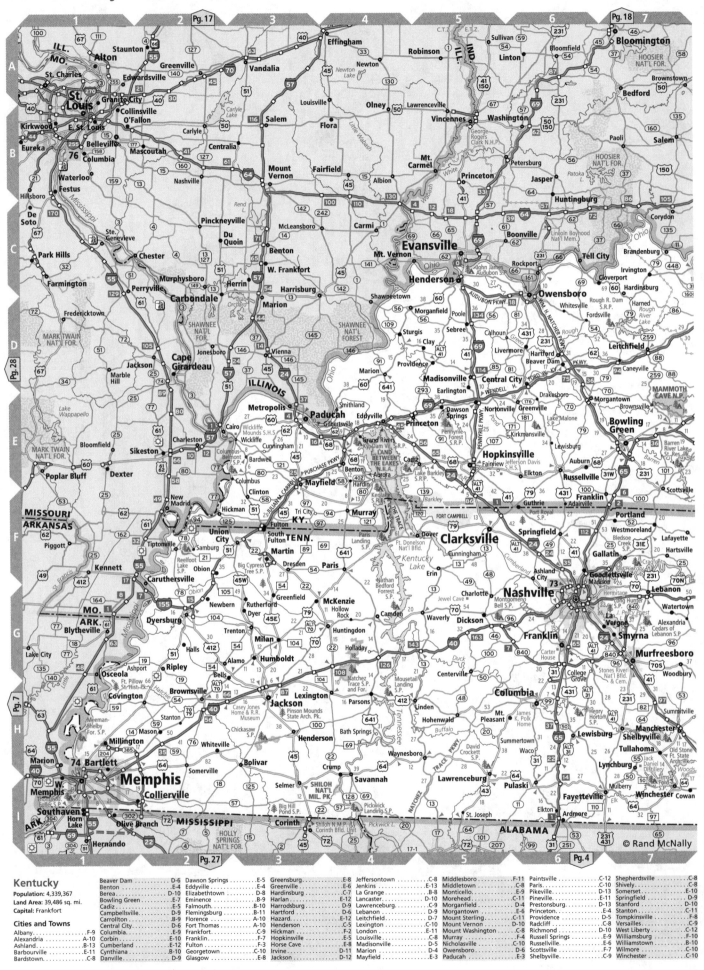

© Rand McNally

NOTE: Maps are not always in alphabetical order.
See Page 1 for map location in this atlas.

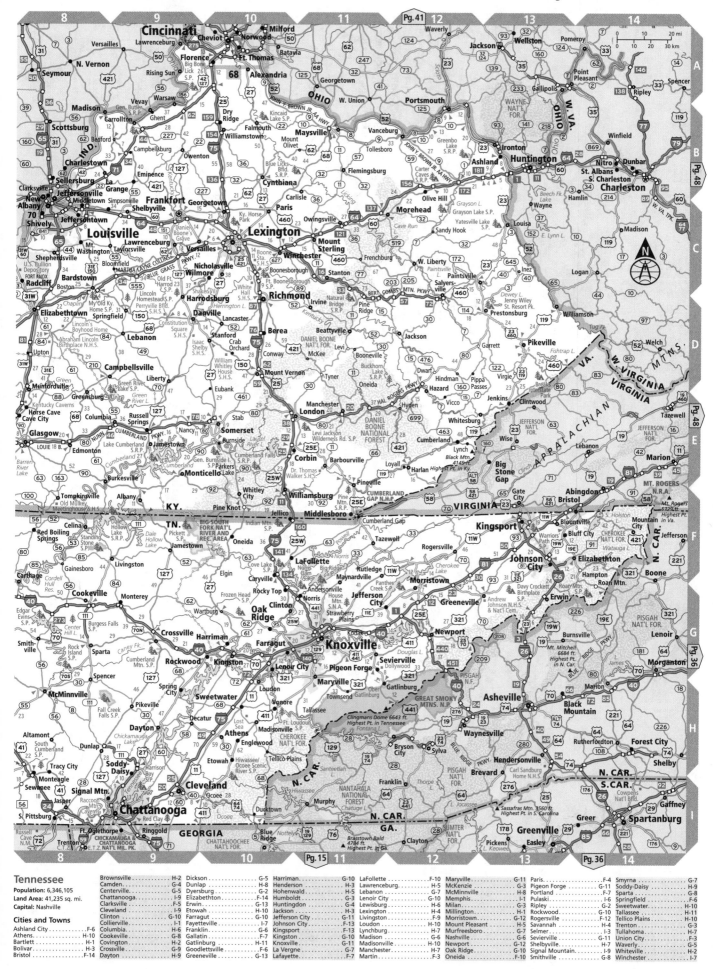

Tennessee

Population: 6,346,105
Land Area: 41,235 sq. mi.
Capital: Nashville

Cities and Towns

Kansas

Population: 2,853,118
Land Area: 81,759 sq. mi.
Capital: Topeka

Cities and Towns

Pg. 28
Pg. 30
Pg. 12
Pg. 42

NEBRASKA

COLORADO

MISSOURI

OKLAHOMA

© Rand McNally

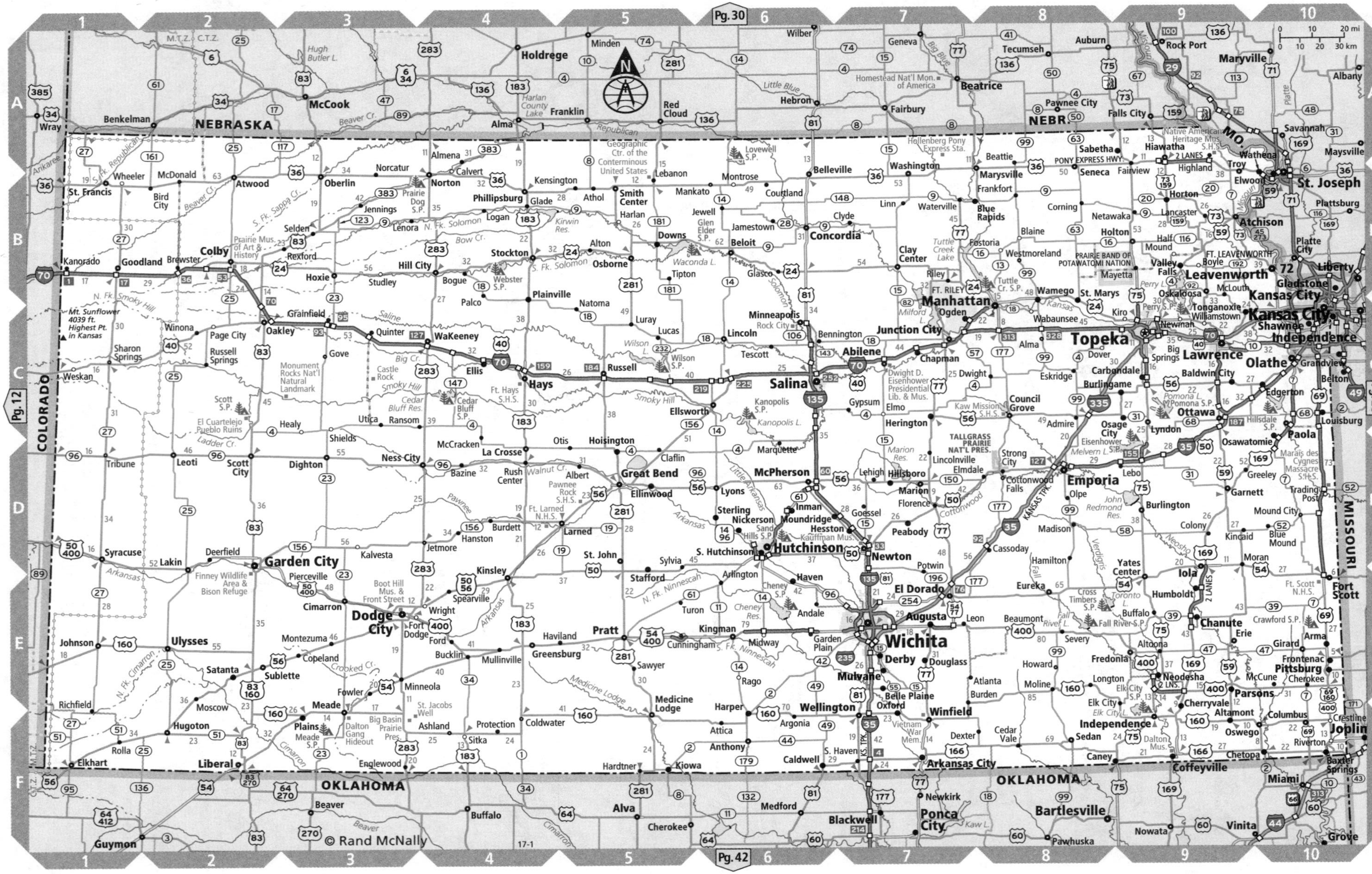

NOTE: Maps are not always in alphabetical order.
See Page 1 for map location in this atlas.

Louisiana 23

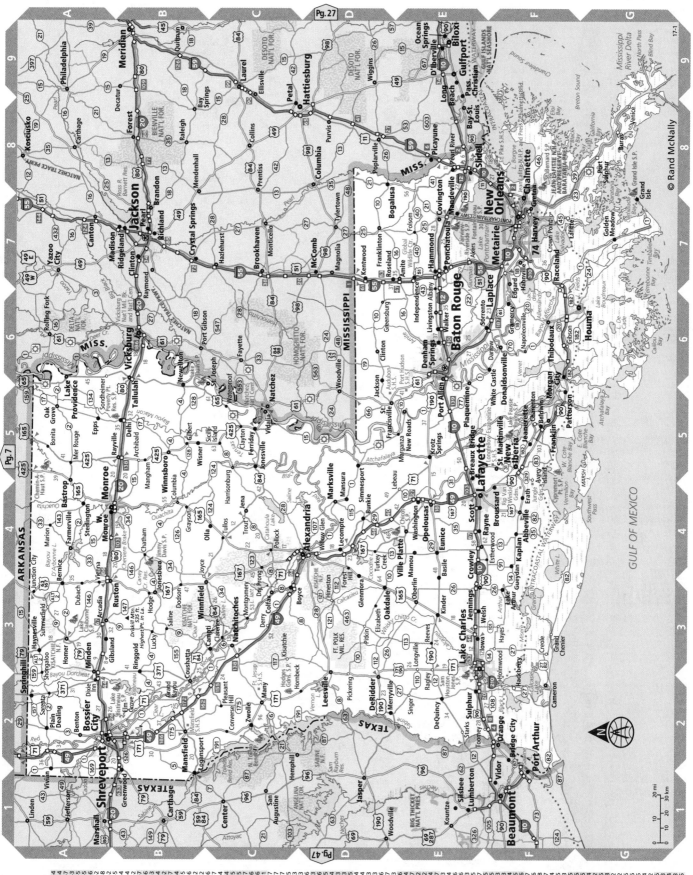

© Rand McNally

Louisiana

Population: 4,533,372
Land Area: 43,204 sq. mi.
Capital: Baton Rouge

17-1

Maine

Population: 1,328,361
Land Area: 30,843 sq. mi.
Capital: Augusta

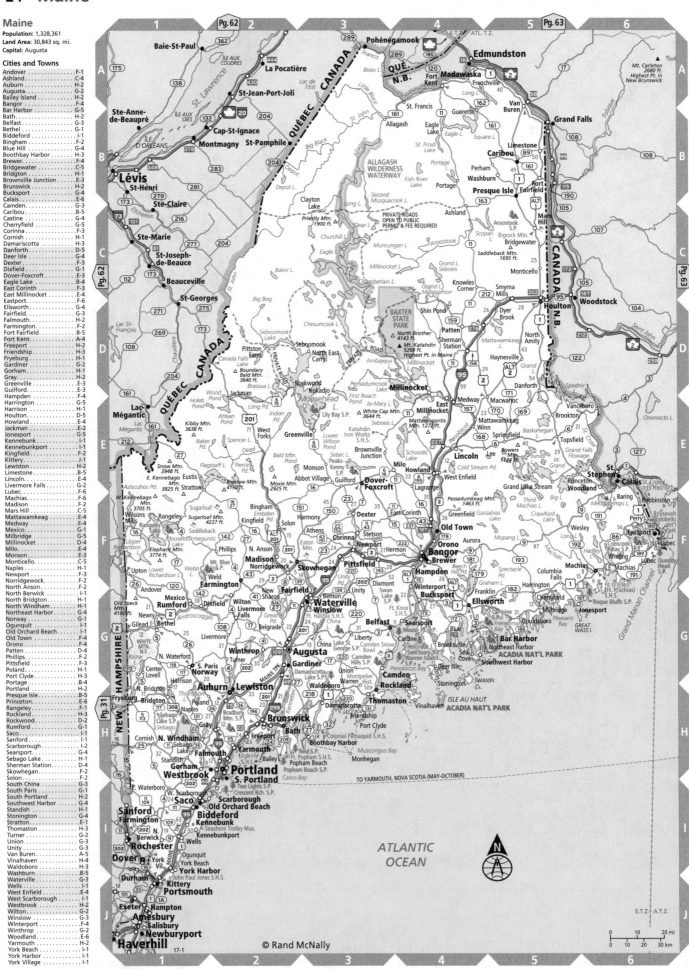

© Rand McNally

17-1

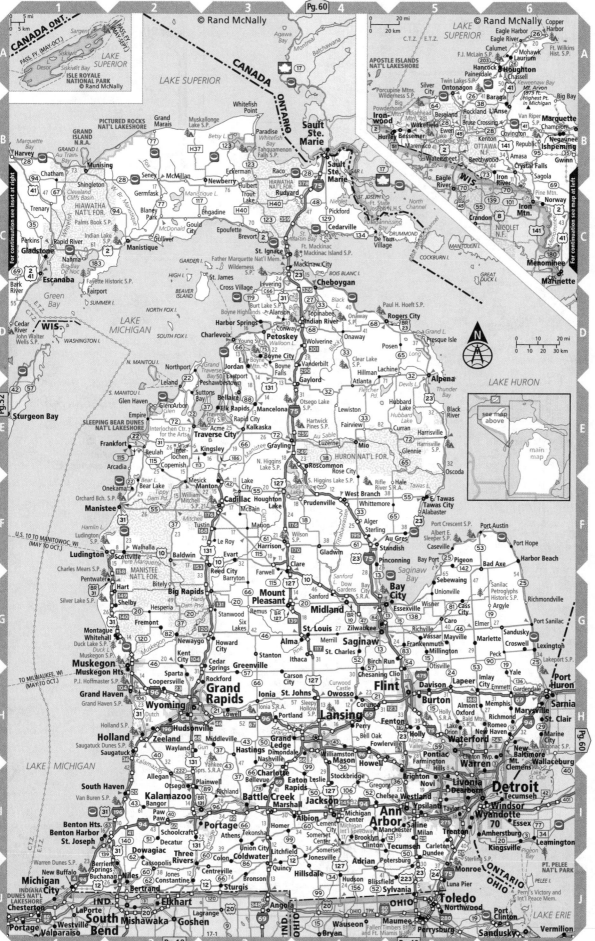

NOTE: Maps are not always in alphabetical order.
See Page 1 for map location in this atlas.

Michigan
Population: 9,883,640
Land Area: 56,539 sq. mi.
Capital: Lansing

Cities and Towns

Minnesota

Population: 5,303,925
Land Area: 79,627 sq. mi.
Capital: St. Paul

Cities and Towns

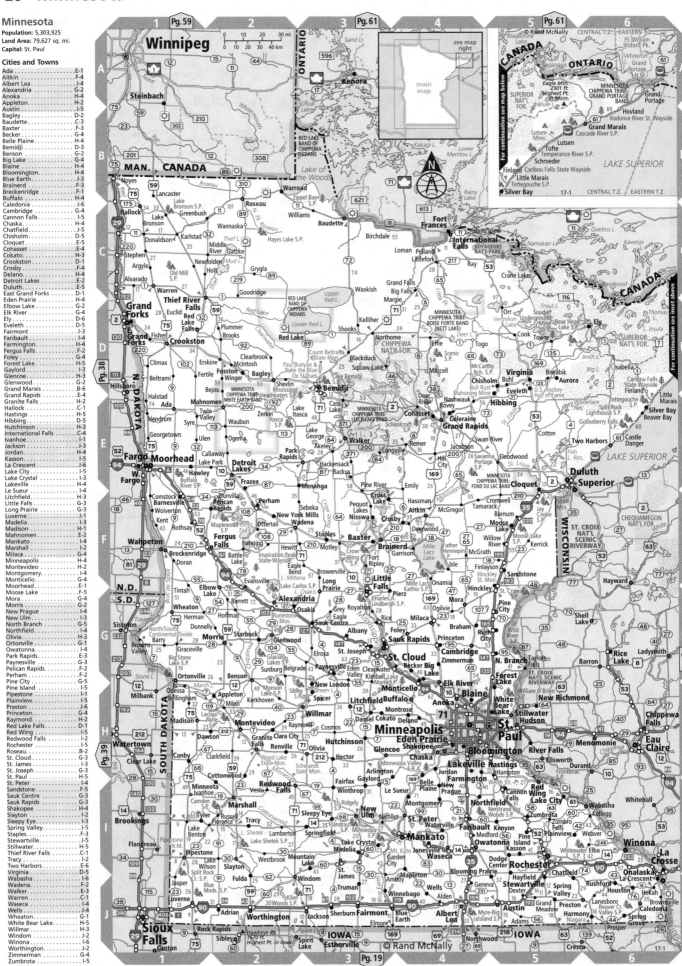

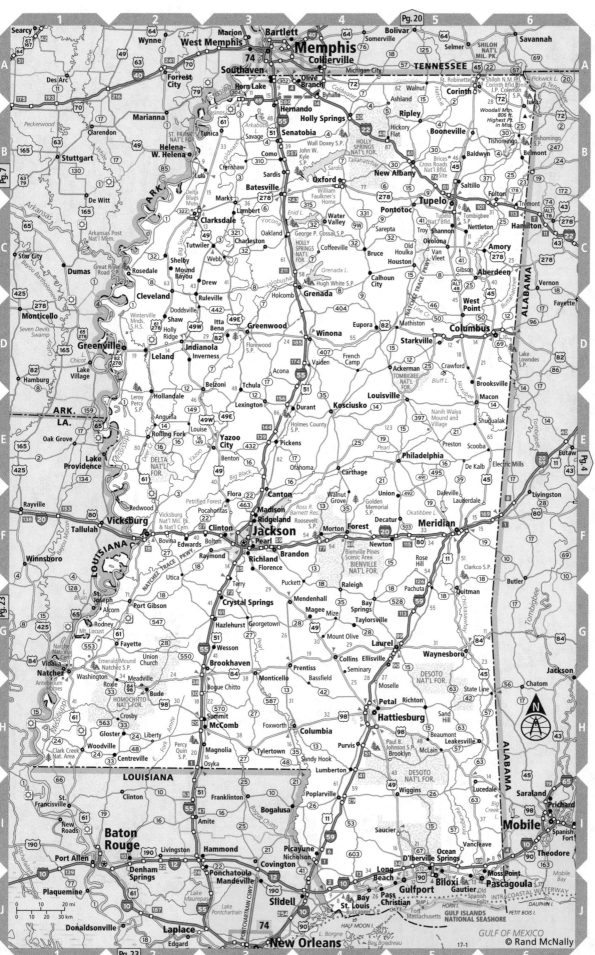

Mississippi
Population: 2,967,297
Land Area: 46,923 sq. mi.
Capital: Jackson

Cities and Towns

© Rand McNally

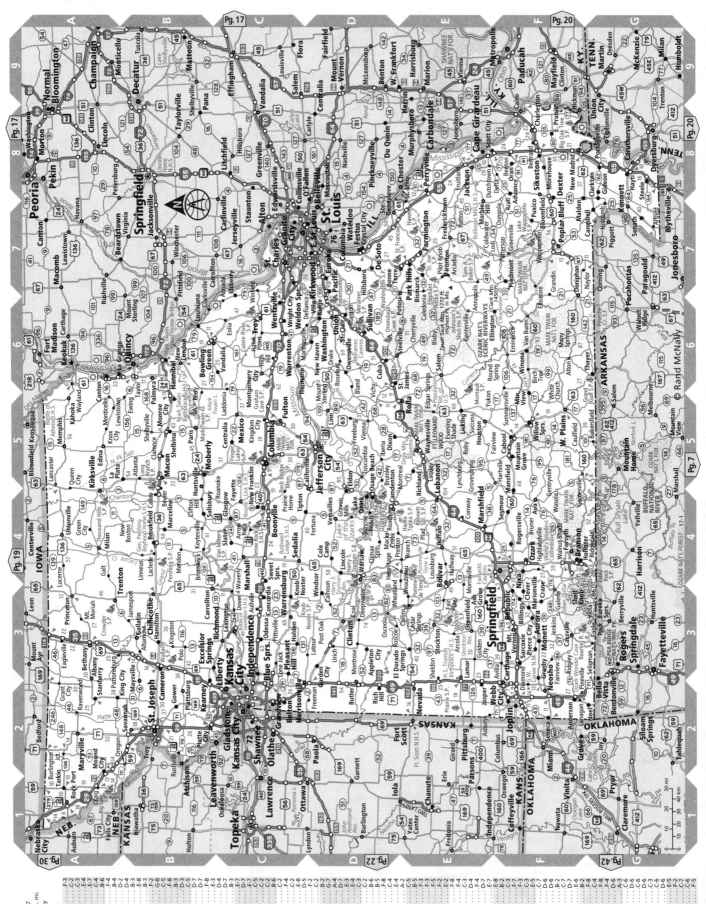

Missouri

Population: 5,988,927
Land Area: 68,741 sq. mi.
Capital: Jefferson City

Cities and Towns

NOTE: Maps are not always in alphabetical order.
See Page 1 for map location in this atlas.

Montana 29

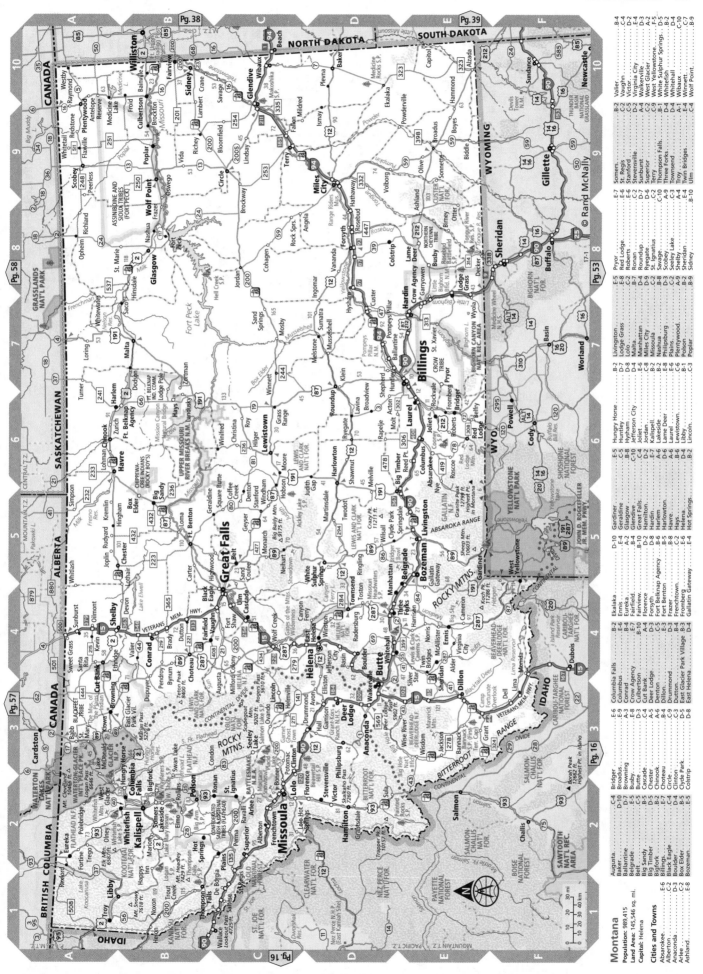

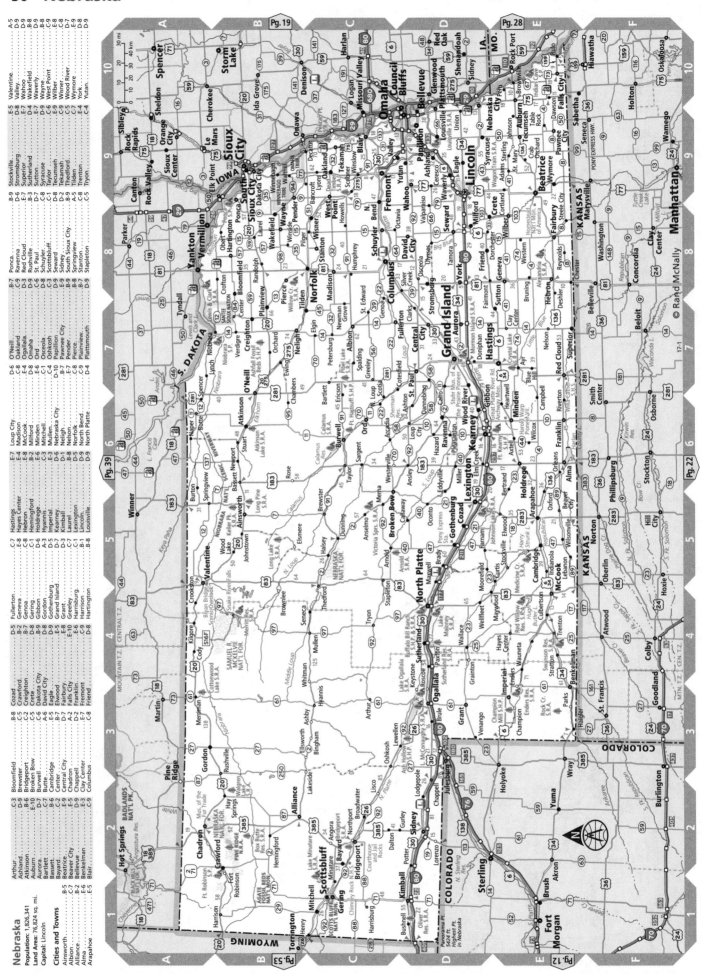

© Rand McNally

NOTE: Maps are not always in alphabetical order.
See Page 1 for map location in this atlas.

© Rand McNally

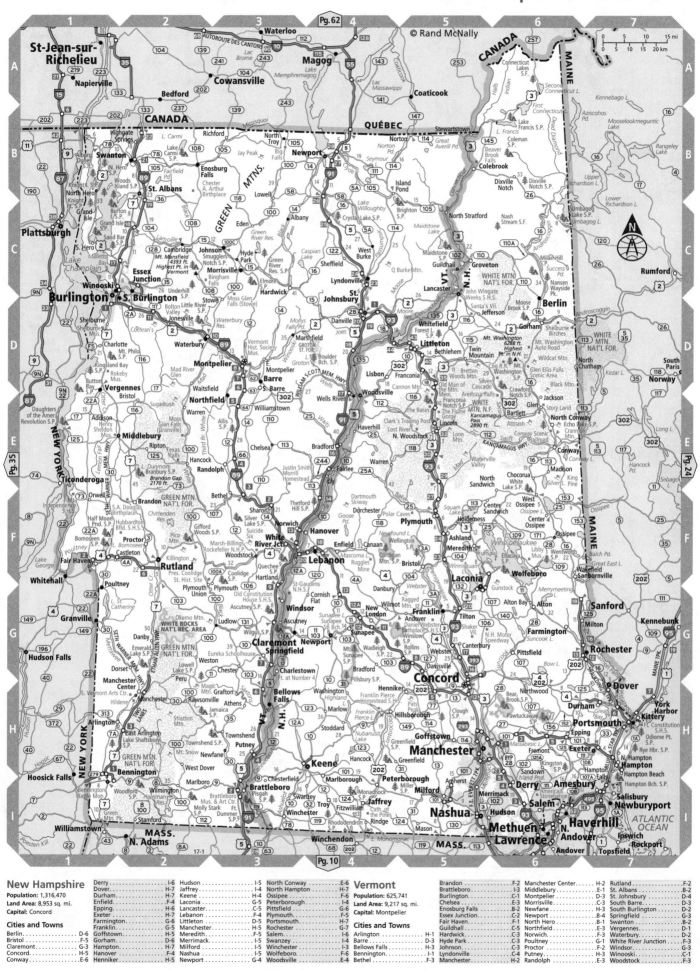

New Jersey
Population: 8,791,894
Land Area: 7,354 sq. mi.
Capital: Trenton

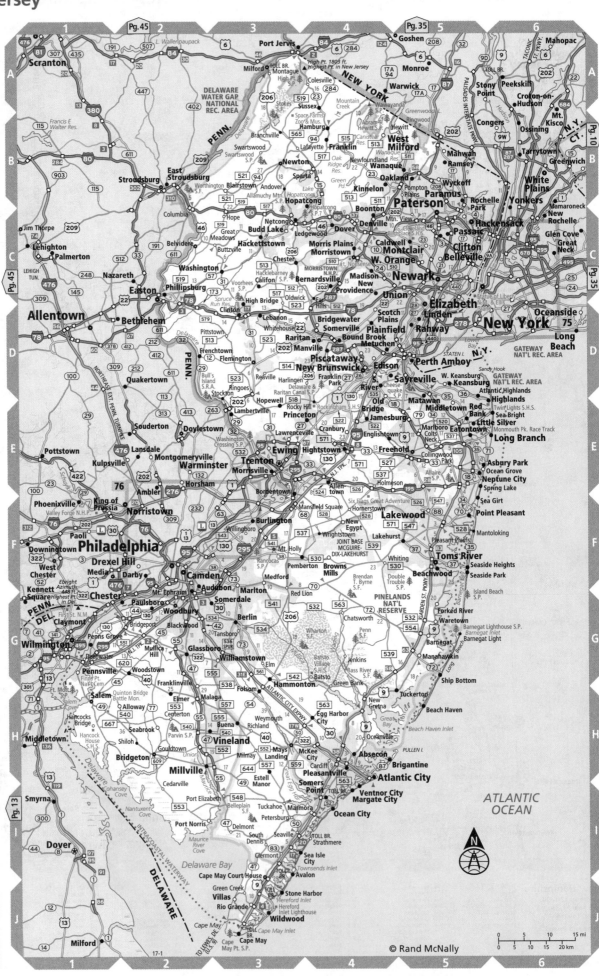

© Rand McNally

NOTE: Maps are not always in alphabetical order.
See Page 1 for map location in this atlas.

New Mexico 33

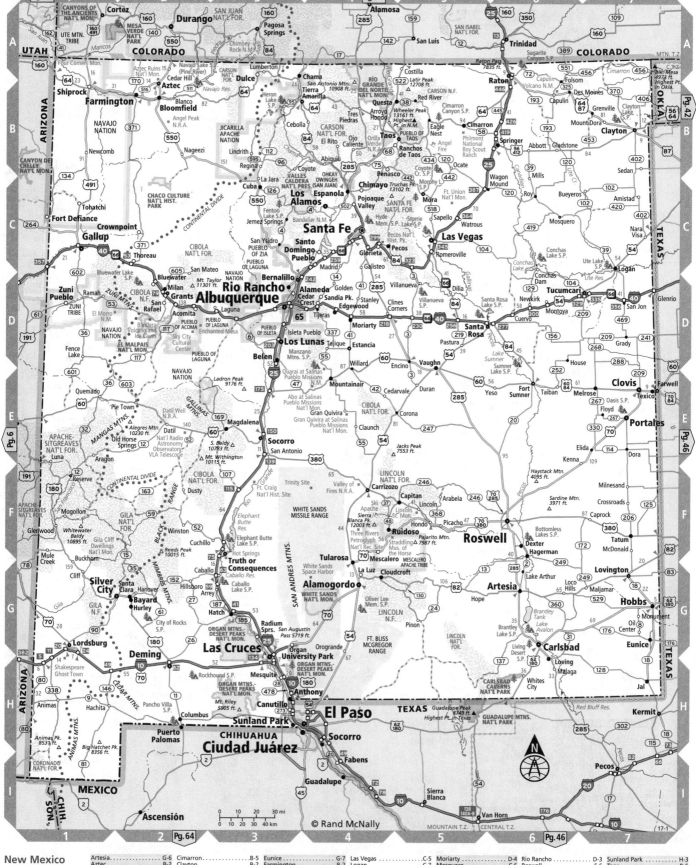

© Rand McNally

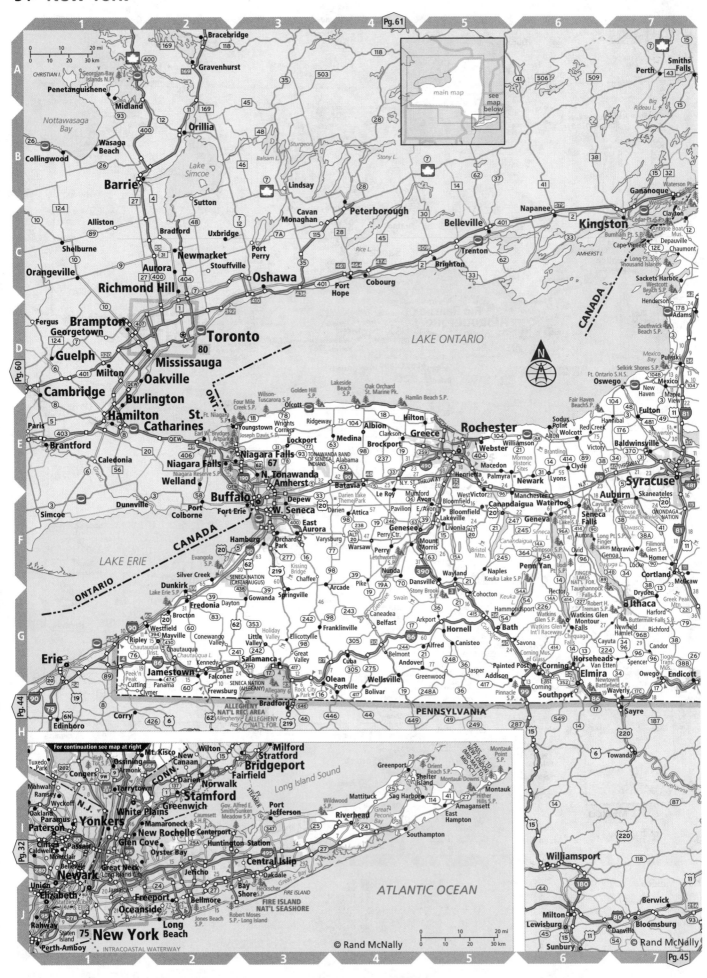

Pg. 61
Pg. 60
Pg. 44
Pg. 32
Pg. 45

© Rand McNally

© Rand McNally

NOTE: Maps are not always in alphabetical order.
See Page 1 for map location in this atlas.

New York 35

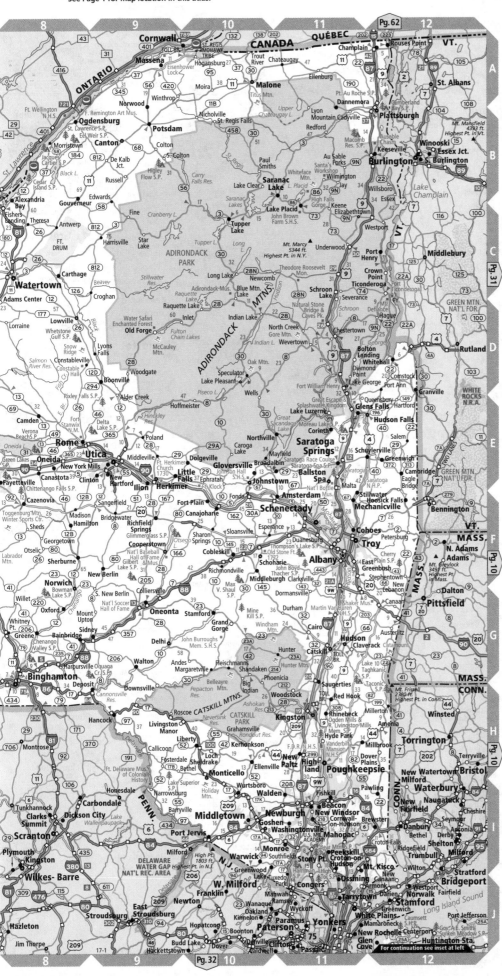

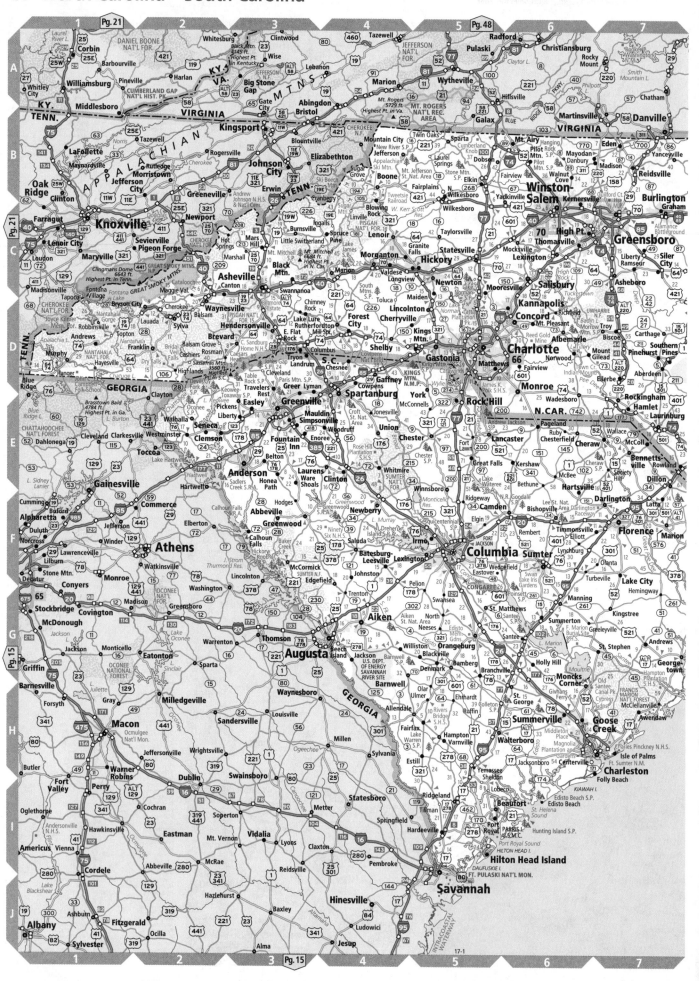

NOTE: Maps are not always in alphabetical order.
See Page 1 for map location in this atlas.

North Carolina • South Carolina   37

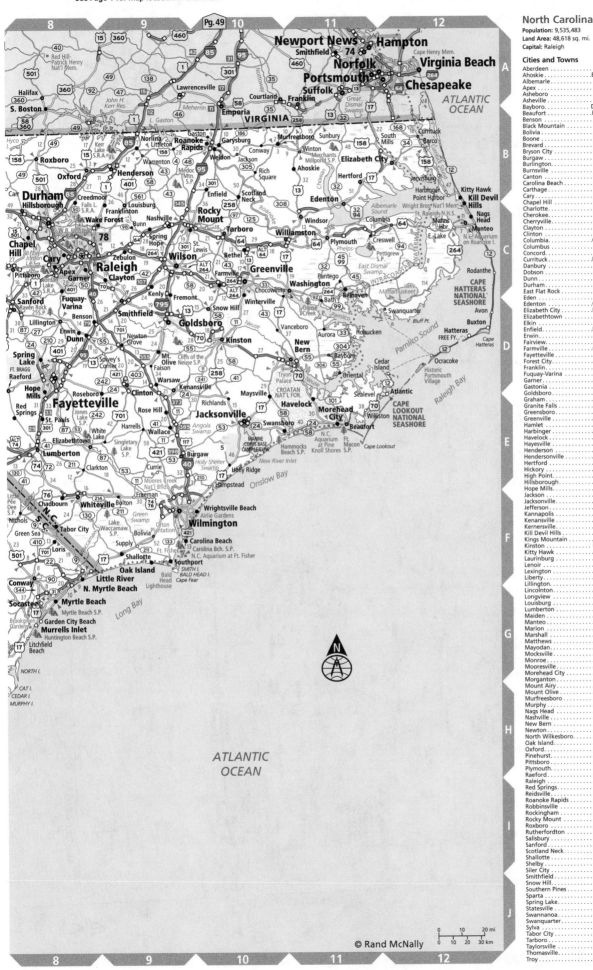

© Rand McNally

North Dakota

Population: 672,591
Land Area: 69,000 sq. mi.
Capital: Bismarck

© Rand McNally

Pg. 26 Pg. 29 Pg. 39 Pg. 58 Pg. 59

NOTE: Maps are not always in alphabetical order.
See Page 1 for map location in this atlas.

South Dakota 39

© Rand McNally

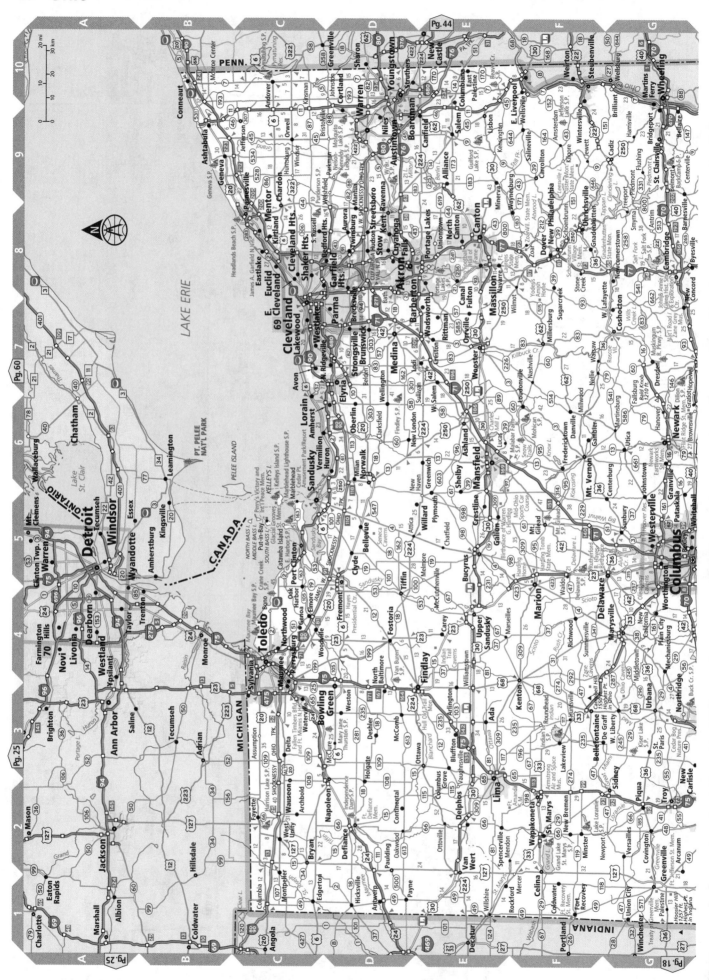

Pg. 44
Pg. 60
Pg. 25
Pg. 25
Pg. 18

NOTE: Maps are not always in alphabetical order.
See Page 1 for map location in this atlas.

Ohio 41

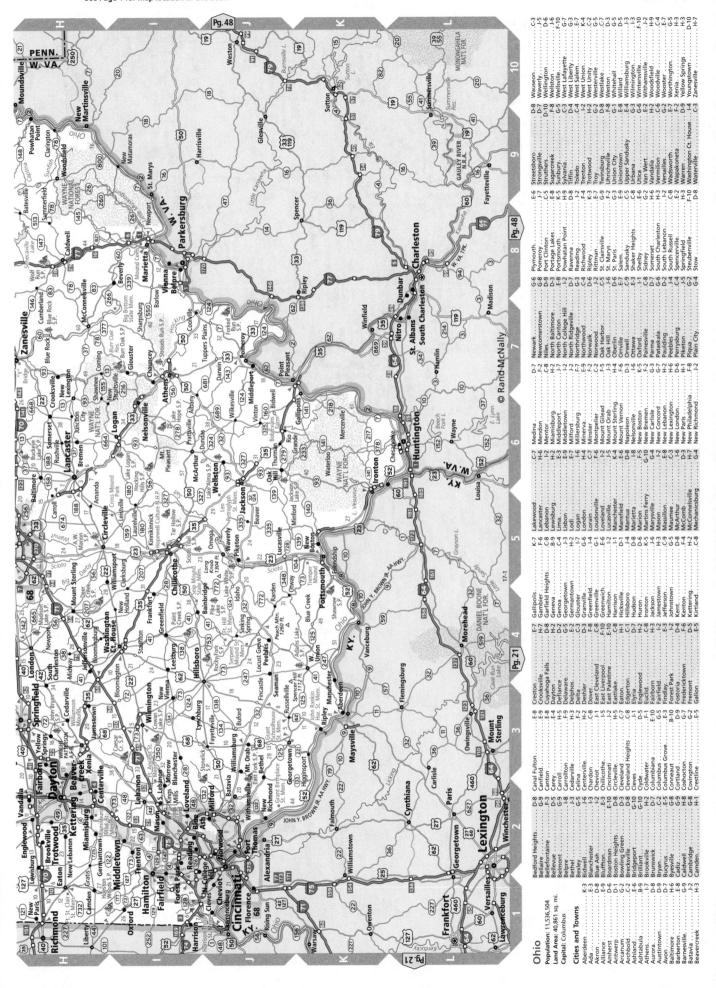

Oklahoma

Population: 3,751,351
Land Area: 68,595 sq. mi.
Capital: Oklahoma City

Cities and Towns

© Rand McNally

NOTE: Maps are not always in alphabetical order.
See Page 1 for map location in this atlas.

Oregon 43

© Rand McNally

PACIFIC OCEAN

WASHINGTON

IDAHO

NEVADA

CALIFORNIA

Oregon

Population: 3,831,074
Land Area: 95,988 sq. mi.
Capital: Salem

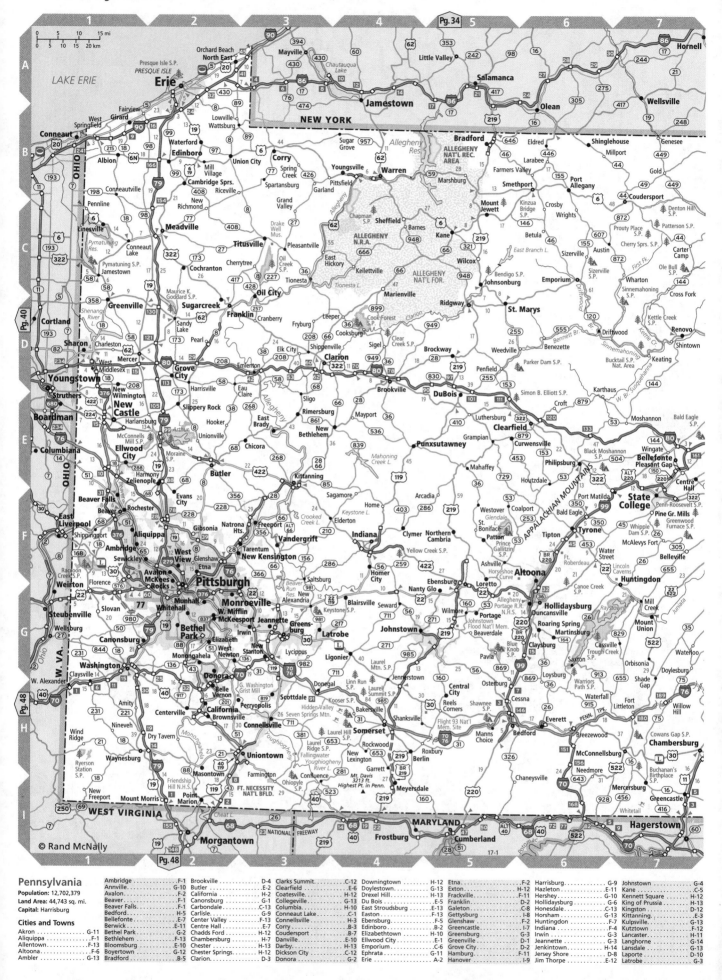

NOTE: Maps are not always in alphabetical order.
See Page 1 for map location in this atlas.

Pennsylvania   45

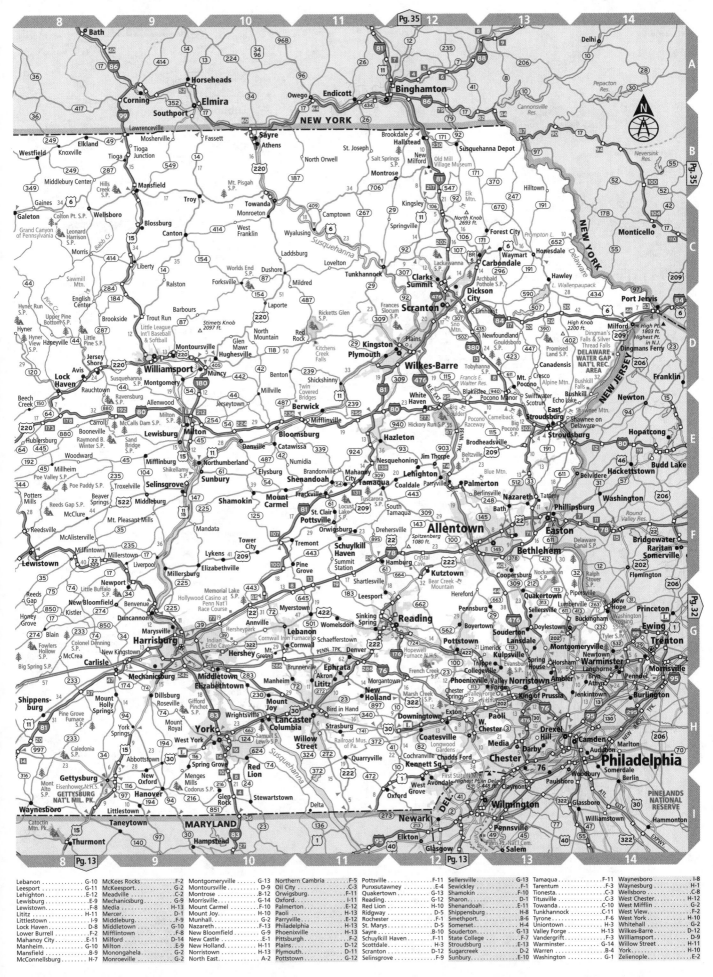

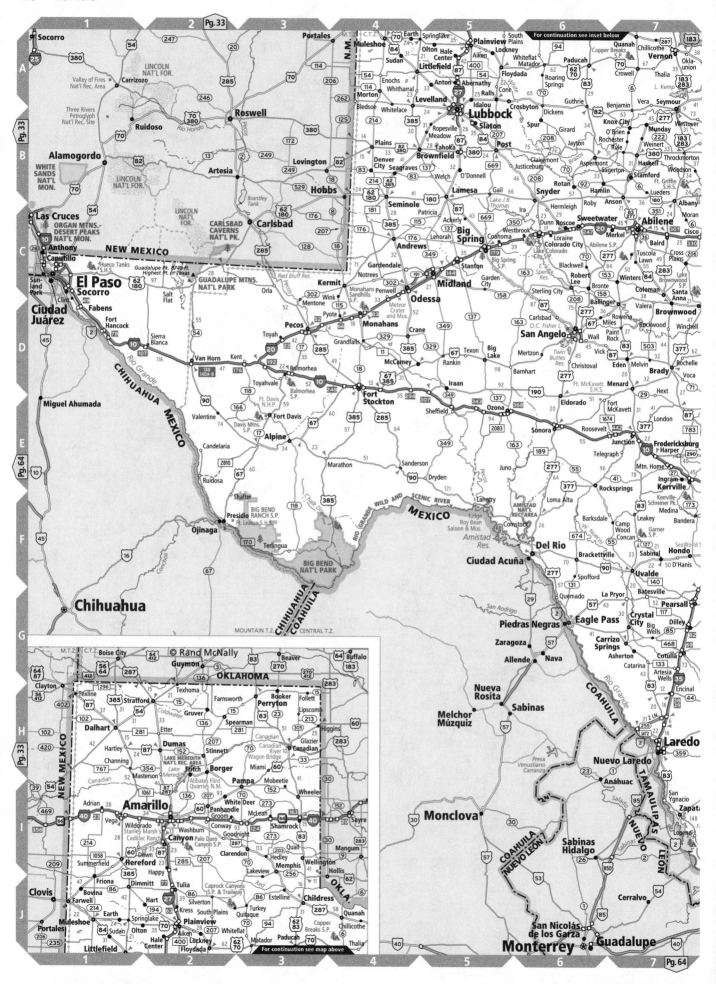

MAP LABELS (left to right, top to bottom):

Socorro · Portales · Earth · Springlake · Plainview · South Plains · Quanah · Chillicothe · Vernon · Okla-union

Carrizozo · Muleshoe · Olton · Hale Center · Lockney · Whiteflat · Matador · Paducah · Crowell · Thalia · L. Kemp

LINCOLN NAT'L FOR. · Sudan · Littlefield · Floydada · Roaring Springs · Benjamin · Vera · Seymour

Valley of Fires Nat'l Rec. Area · Enochs · Whitharral · Anton · Abernathy · Cone · Guthrie · Knox City · O'Brien · Westover

Three Rivers Petroglyph Nat'l Rec. Site · Roswell · Morton · Whiteface · Levelland · Ralls · Crosbyton · Dickens · Rochester · Weinert · Munday

Ruidoso · Rio Hondo · Bledsoe · Lubbock · Slaton · Spur · Jayton · Girard · Aspermont · Sagerton · Haskell · Woodson

Alamogordo · WHITE SANDS NAT'L MON. · Plains · Tahoka · Post · Clairemont · Justiceburg · Rotan · Hamlin · Stamford · Ft. Griffin S.H.S.

Las Cruces · ORGAN MTNS.-DESERT PEAKS NAT'L MON. · Artesia · Lovington · Denver City · Seagraves · Brownfield · Welch · O'Donnell · Snyder · Anson · Albany

Anthony · Canutillo · Hobbs · Seminole · Lamesa · Ira · Hermleigh · Roby · Sweetwater · Merkel · Abilene · Baird · Cisco

El Paso · Socorro · Carlsbad · CARLSBAD CAVERNS NAT'L PK. · Andrews · Ackerly · Big Spring · Coahoma · Colorado City · Blackwell · Winters · Coleman · Santa Anna

Ciudad Juárez · Fabens · Fort Hancock · Kermit · Gardendale · Notrees · Stanton · Midland · Garden City · Sterling City · Bronte · Miles · Rockwood · Winchell · Brownwood

Sierra Blanca · Van Horn · Kent · Pecos · Toyah · Wink · Pyote · Monahans · Odessa · Crane · Big Lake · Mertzon · Valera · Brady

Miguel Ahumada · Balmorhea · McCamey · Rankin · Barnhart · San Angelo · Wall · Paint Rock · Eden · Melvin · Rochelle · Voca

CHIHUAHUA MEXICO · Toyahvale · Fort Stockton · Iraan · Ozona · Eldorado · Fort McKavett S.H.S. · Menard · Hext · Brady

Valentine · Ft. Davis N.H.P. · Alpine · Marathon · Sheffield · Sonora · Roosevelt · Junction · Fredericksburg · Harper

Candelaria · Davis Mtns. S.P. · Fort Davis · Sanderson · Dryden · Juno · Telegraph · Mtn. Home · Ingram · Kerrville

Ruidosa · Shafter · Presidio · BIG BEND RANCH S.P. · Langtry · AMISTAD NAT'L REC. AREA · Rocksprings · Loma Alta · Leakey · Medina · Bandera

Ojinaga · Terlingua · BIG BEND NAT'L PARK · Judge Roy Bean Saloon & Mus. · Amistad Res. · Comstock · Barksdale · Camp Wood · Concan · Garner S.P.

Chihuahua · MEXICO · Del Rio · Ciudad Acuña · Brackettville · Spofford · Hondo · D'Hanis · Uvalde · SeaWorld

Piedras Negras · Eagle Pass · La Pryor · Batesville · Pearsall · Crystal City · Big Wells · Dilley

Zaragoza · Allende · Nava · Quemado · Carrizo Springs · Asherton · Cotulla · Catarina · Artesia Wells · Encinal

Nueva Rosita · Sabinas · Encinal · Laredo · Nuevo Laredo

Melchor Múzquiz · Presa Venustiano Carranza · Anáhuac · San Ygnacio · Zapata

Monclova · Sabinas Hidalgo · Cerralvo

San Nicolás de los Garza · Monterrey · Guadalupe

INSET MAP (lower left):

© Rand McNally · Boise City · Beaver · Buffalo · Clayton · Guymon · OKLAHOMA · Texline · Texhoma · Farnsworth · Booker · Follett · Lipscomb

Stratford · Gruver · Perryton · Spearman · Higgins · Dalhart · Hartley · Dumas · Stinnett · Glazier · Canadian

Channing · Borger · Fritch · Miami · Mobeetie · Wheeler · LAKE MEREDITH NAT'L REC. AREA · Pampa · McLean · Shamrock · Sayre

Adrian · Vega · Amarillo · White Deer · Panhandle · Groom · Wellington · Hollis

Wildorado · Canyon · Conway · Goodnight · Clarendon · Hedley · Memphis · PALO DURO CANYON S.P. · CAPROCK CANYONS S.P.

Hereford · Happy · Tulia · Silverton · Turkey · Quitaque · Childress · Quanah · Chillicothe

Clovis · Bovina · Farwell · Hart · Kress · South Plains · Whiteflat · Paducah · Thalia

Portales · Muleshoe · Sudan · Olton · Hale Center · Floydada · Lockney · Matador

Littlefield · Springlake · Plainview

NOTE: Maps are not always in alphabetical order.
See Page 1 for map location in this atlas.

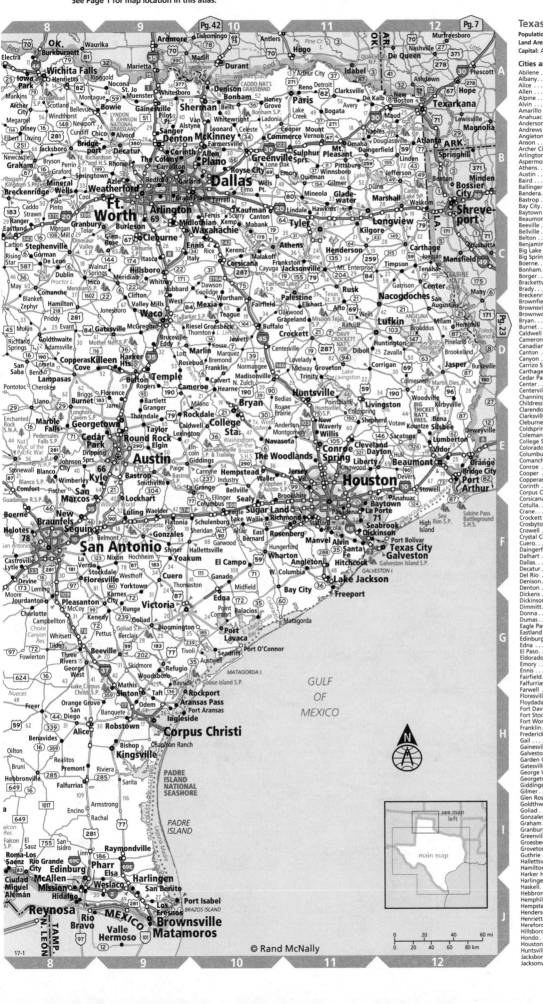

© Rand McNally

Texas

Population: 25,145,561
Land Area: 261,231 sq. mi.
Capital: Austin

Cities and Towns

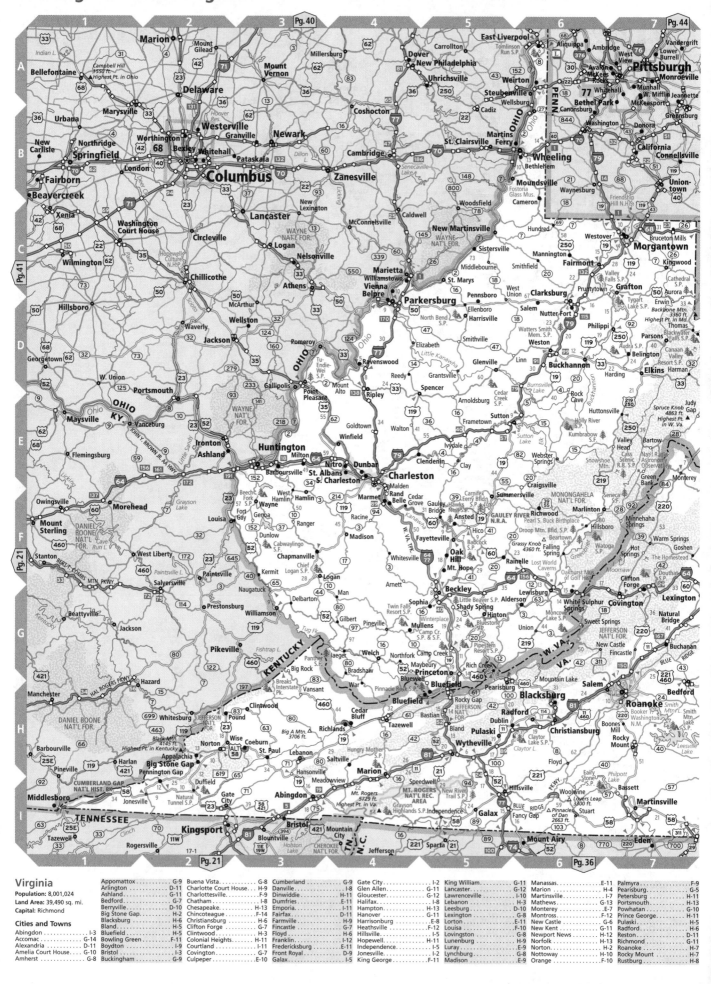

NOTE: Maps are not always in alphabetical order.
See Page 1 for map location in this atlas.

Virginia • West Virginia 49

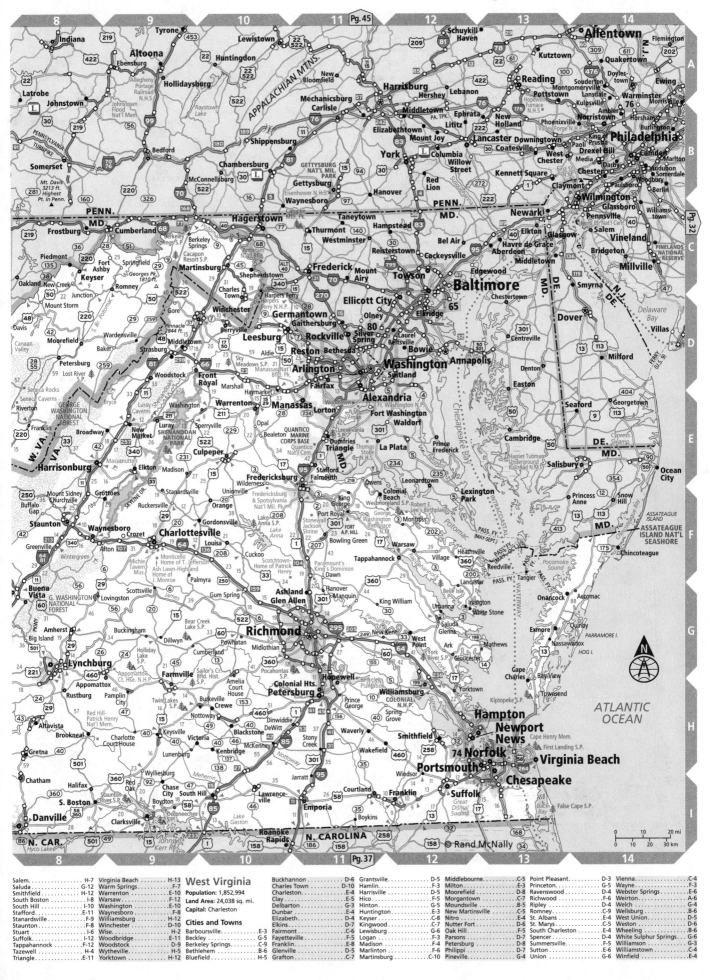

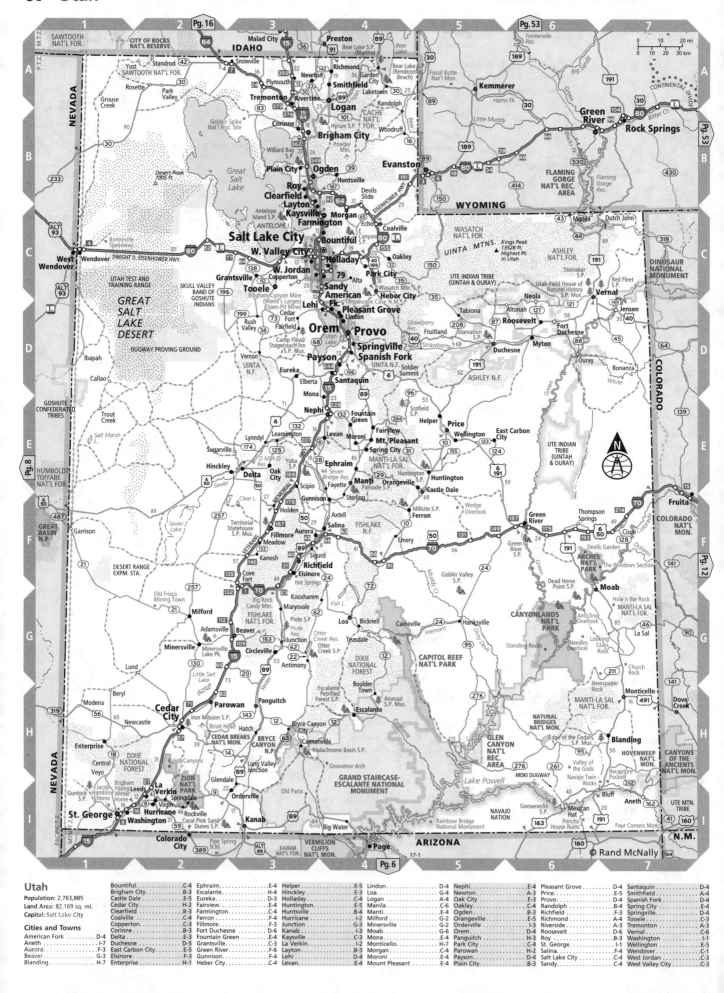

© Rand McNally

Utah

Population: 2,763,885
Land Area: 82,169 sq. mi.
Capital: Salt Lake City

Cities and Towns

NOTE: Maps are not always in alphabetical order.
See Page 1 for map location in this atlas.

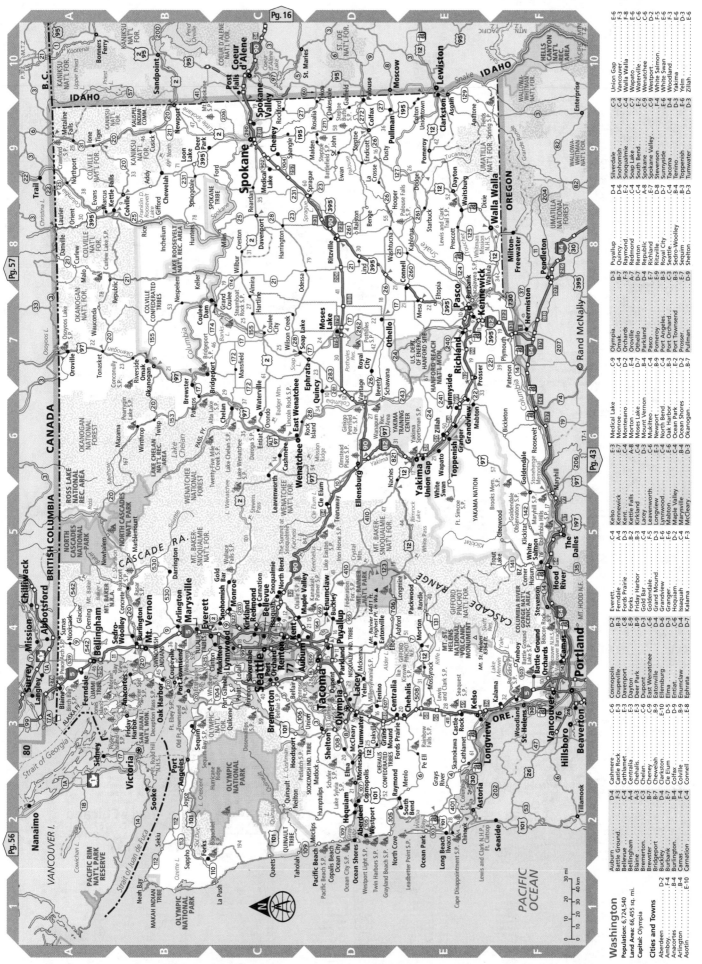

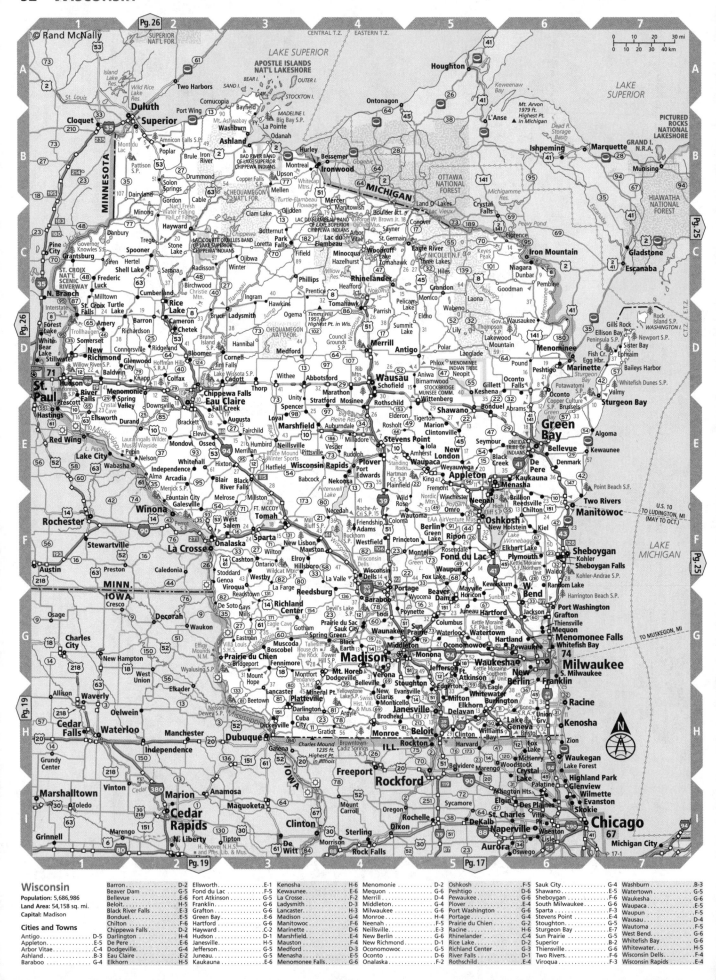

© Rand McNally

NOTE: Maps are not always in alphabetical order.
See Page 1 for map location in this atlas.

Wyoming   53

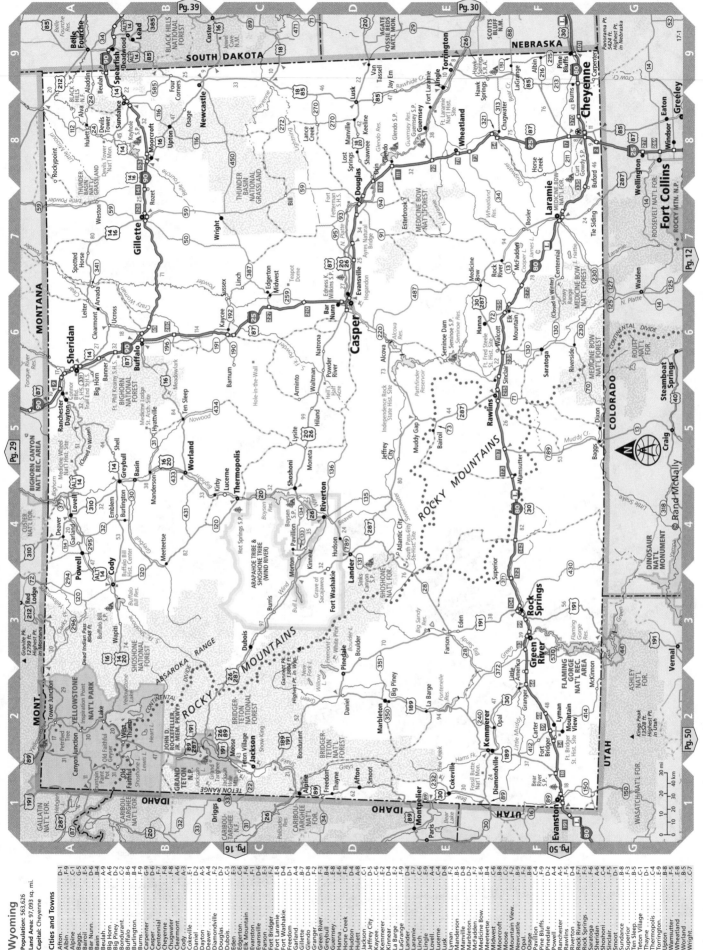

Pg. 39   Pg. 30   Pg. 29   Pg. 12   Pg. 50   Pg. 16   Pg. 50

Wyoming

Population: 563,626
Land Area: 97,093 sq. mi.
Capital: Cheyenne

Cities and Towns

Ottawa (inset map)

© Rand McNally

17-1

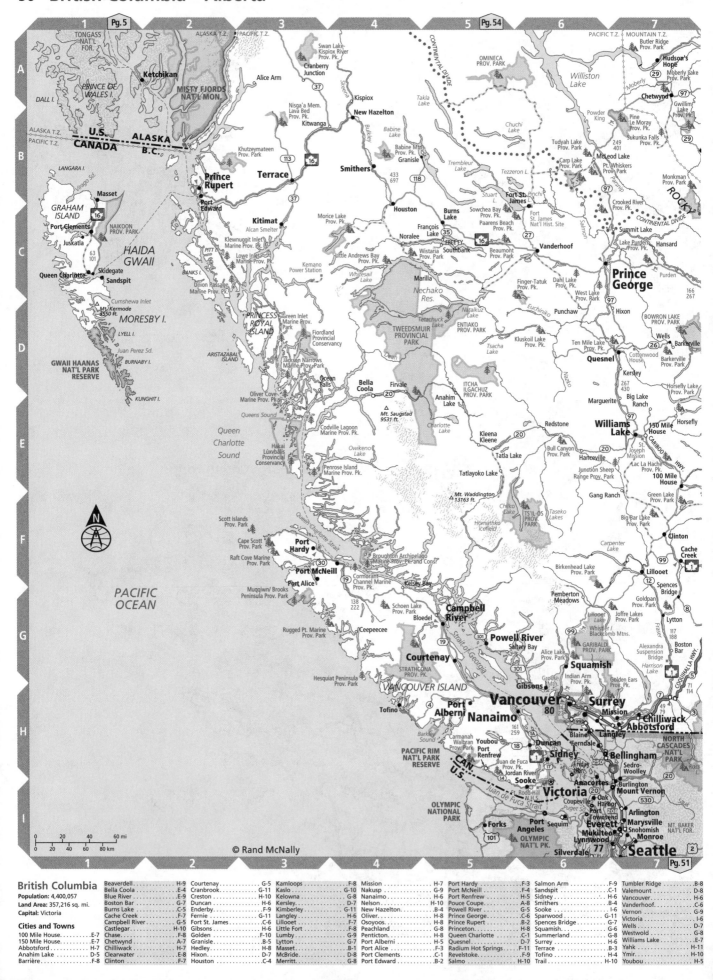

© Rand McNally

NOTE: Maps are not always in alphabetical order.
See Page 1 for map location in this atlas.

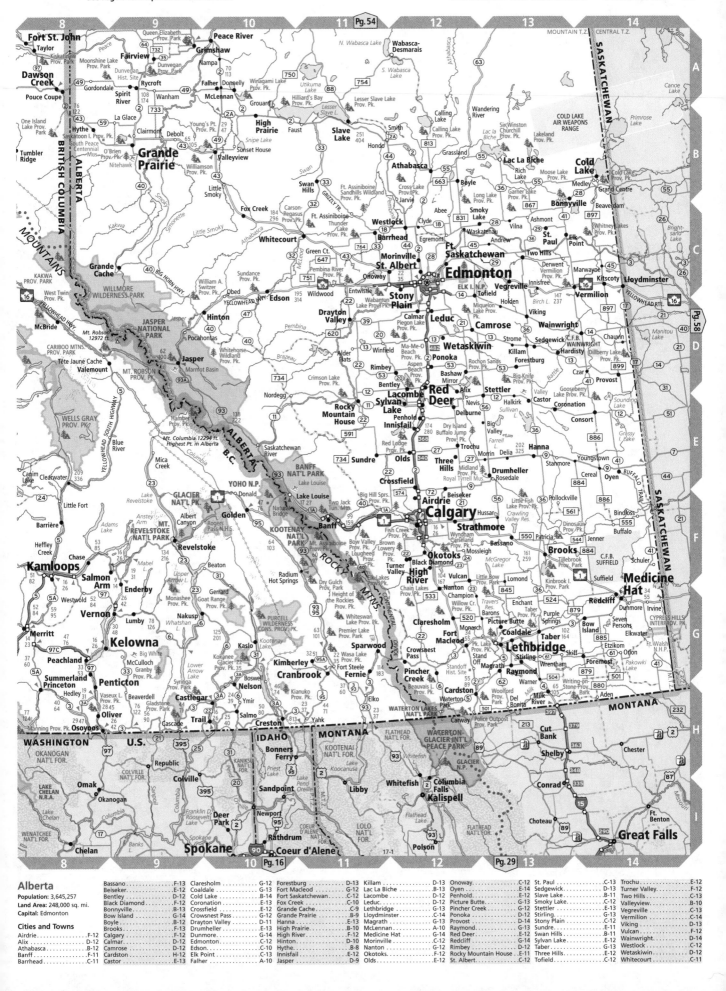

Alberta

Population: 3,645,257
Land Area: 248,000 sq. mi.
Capital: Edmonton

Cities and Towns

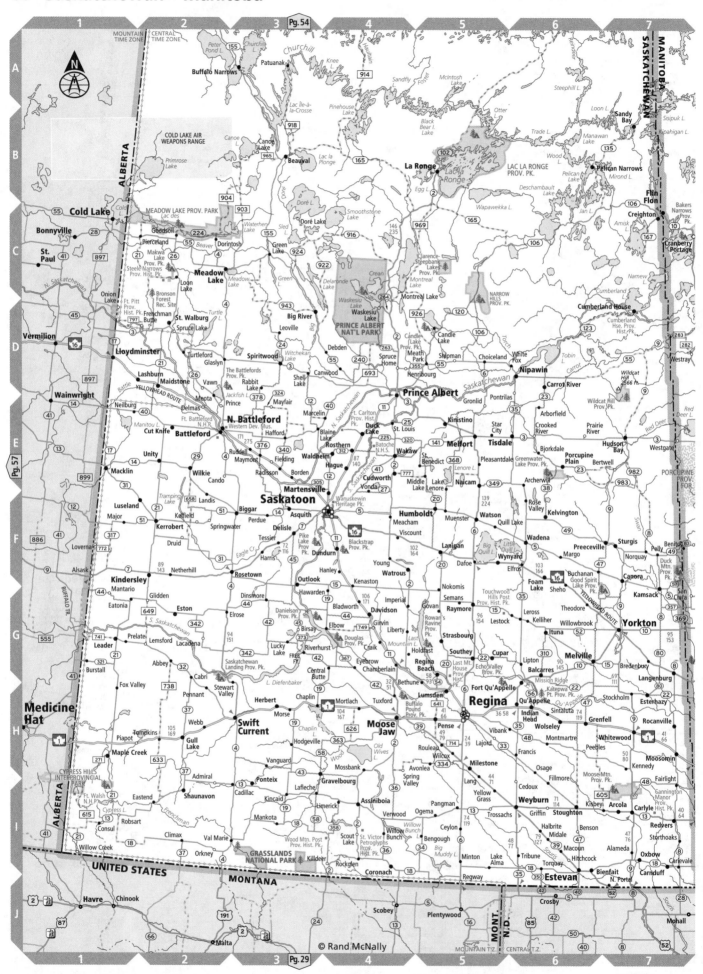

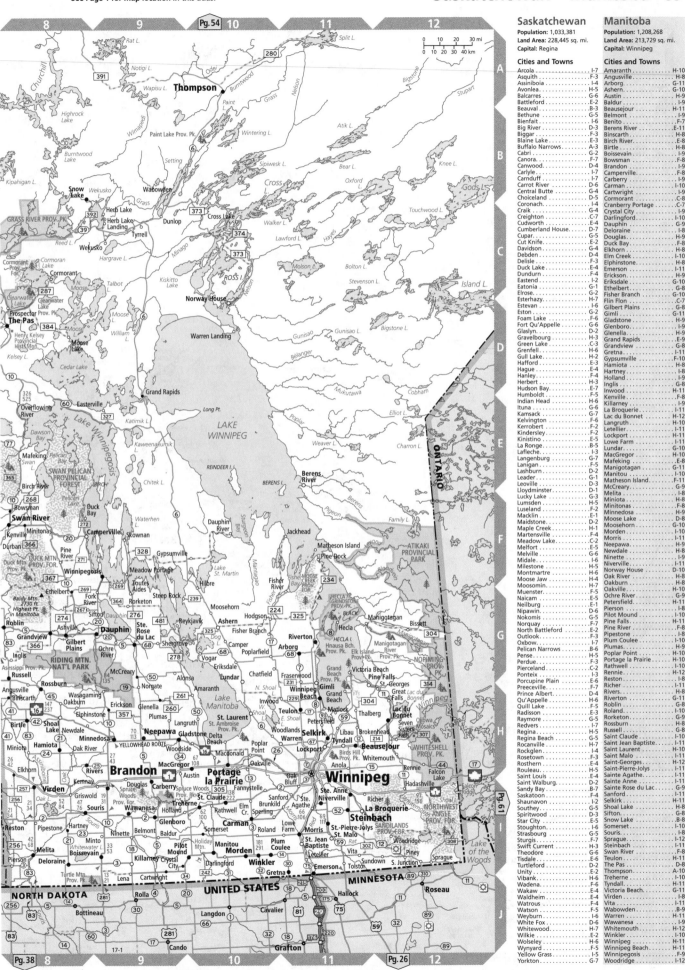

NOTE: Maps are not always in alphabetical order.
See Page 1 for map location in this atlas.

Saskatchewan
Population: 1,033,381
Land Area: 228,445 sq. mi.
Capital: Regina

Cities and Towns

Arcola	I-7
Asquith	F-3
Assiniboia	I-4
Avonlea	H-5
Balcarres	G-6
Battleford	E-2
Beauval	B-3
Bethune	H-5
Bienfait	I-6
Big River	D-3
Biggar	F-3
Blaine Lake	E-3
Buffalo Narrows	A-3
Cabri	G-2
Canora	F-7
Canwood	D-4
Carlyle	I-7
Carnduff	I-7
Carrot River	D-6
Central Butte	H-4
Choiceland	D-5
Coronach	I-4
Craik	G-4
Creighton	C-7
Cudworth	E-4
Cumberland House	D-7
Cupar	G-5
Cut Knife	E-2
Davidson	G-4
Debden	D-4
Delisle	F-3
Duck Lake	E-4
Dundurn	F-4
Eastend	I-2
Eatonia	G-1
Elrose	G-2
Esterhazy	H-7
Estevan	I-6
Eston	G-2
Foam Lake	F-6
Fort Qu'Appelle	H-6
Glaslyn	D-2
Gravelbourg	H-3
Green Lake	C-3
Grenfell	H-6
Gull Lake	H-2
Hafford	E-3
Hague	E-4
Hanley	F-4
Herbert	H-3
Hudson Bay	E-7
Humboldt	F-5
Indian Head	H-6
Ituna	G-6
Kamsack	G-7
Kelvington	F-6
Kerrobert	F-2
Kindersley	F-2
Kinistino	E-5
La Ronge	B-5
Lafleche	I-3
Langenburg	G-7
Lanigan	F-5
Lashburn	D-2
Leader	G-1
Leoville	D-3
Lloydminster	D-1
Lucky Lake	G-3
Lumsden	H-5
Luseland	F-2
Macklin	E-1
Maidstone	D-2
Maple Creek	H-1
Martensville	F-4
Meadow Lake	C-2
Melfort	E-5
Melville	G-6
Midale	I-6
Milestone	H-5
Montmartre	H-6
Moose Jaw	H-4
Moosomin	H-7
Muenster	F-5
Naicam	E-5
Neilburg	E-1
Nipawin	D-6
Nokomis	G-5
Norquay	F-7
North Battleford	E-2
Outlook	F-3
Oxbow	I-7
Pelican Narrows	B-6
Pense	H-5
Perdue	F-3
Pierceland	C-2
Pontiex	I-3
Porcupine Plain	E-6
Preeceville	F-7
Prince Albert	D-4
Qu'Appelle	H-6
Quill Lake	F-5
Radisson	E-3
Raymore	G-5
Redvers	I-7
Regina	H-5
Regina Beach	G-5
Rocanville	H-7
Rockglen	I-4
Rosetown	F-3
Rosthern	E-4
Rouleau	H-5
Saint Louis	E-4
Saint Walburg	D-2
Sandy Bay	B-7
Saskatoon	F-4
Shaunavon	I-2
Southey	G-5
Spiritwood	D-3
Star City	E-5
Stoughton	I-6
Strasbourg	G-5
Sturgis	F-7
Swift Current	H-3
Theodore	G-6
Tisdale	E-6
Turtleford	D-2
Unity	E-2
Vibank	H-6
Wadena	F-6
Wakaw	E-4
Waldheim	E-4
Watrous	F-4
Watson	F-5
Weyburn	I-6
White Fox	D-6
Whitewood	H-7
Wilkie	E-2
Wolseley	H-6
Wynyard	F-5
Yellow Grass	I-5
Yorkton	G-7

Manitoba
Population: 1,208,268
Land Area: 213,729 sq. mi.
Capital: Winnipeg

Cities and Towns

Amaranth	H-10
Angusville	H-8
Arborg	G-11
Ashern	G-10
Austin	H-9
Baldur	I-9
Beausejour	H-11
Belmont	I-9
Benito	F-7
Berens River	E-11
Binscarth	H-8
Birch River	E-8
Birtle	H-8
Boissevain	I-9
Bowsman	F-8
Brandon	I-9
Camperville	F-8
Carberry	I-9
Carman	I-9
Cartwright	I-9
Cormorant	C-8
Cranberry Portage	C-7
Crystal City	I-9
Darlingford	I-10
Dauphin	G-9
Deloraine	I-9
Douglas	H-9
Duck Bay	F-8
Elkhorn	H-8
Elm Creek	I-10
Elphinstone	H-8
Emerson	I-11
Erickson	H-9
Eriksdale	G-10
Ethelbert	G-8
Fisher Branch	G-10
Flin Flon	C-7
Gilbert Plains	G-8
Gimli	G-11
Gladstone	I-9
Glenboro	I-9
Glenella	H-9
Grand Rapids	E-9
Grandview	H-8
Gretna	I-11
Gypsumville	F-10
Hamiota	H-8
Hartney	I-8
Holland	I-9
Inglis	G-8
Inwood	H-11
Kenville	F-8
Killarney	I-9
La Broquerie	I-11
Lac du Bonnet	H-12
Langruth	H-10
Letellier	I-11
Lockport	H-11
Lowe Farm	I-11
Lundar	G-10
MacGregor	H-10
Mafeking	E-8
Manigotagan	G-11
Manitou	I-10
Matheson Island	F-11
McCreary	G-9
Melita	I-8
Minitonas	F-8
Minnedosa	H-9
Moose Lake	D-8
Moosehorn	G-10
Morden	I-10
Morris	I-11
Neepawa	H-9
Newdale	H-8
Ninette	I-9
Niverville	I-11
Norway House	D-10
Oak River	H-8
Oakburn	H-8
Oakville	H-10
Ochre River	G-9
Petersfield	H-11
Pierson	I-8
Pilot Mound	I-9
Pine Falls	H-11
Pine River	F-8
Pipestone	I-8
Plum Coulee	I-10
Plumas	H-9
Poplar Point	H-10
Portage la Prairie	I-10
Rathwell	I-10
Rennie	H-12
Reston	I-8
Richer	I-11
Rivers	H-8
Riverton	G-11
Roblin	G-8
Roland	I-10
Rorketon	G-9
Rossburn	H-8
Russell	H-8
Saint Claude	I-10
Saint Jean Baptiste	I-11
Saint Laurent	H-10
Saint Malo	I-11
Saint-Georges	H-12
Saint-Pierre-Jolys	I-11
Sainte Agathe	I-11
Sainte Anne	I-11
Sainte Rose du Lac	G-9
Sanford	I-10
Selkirk	H-11
Shoal Lake	H-8
Sifton	G-9
Snow Lake	B-8
Somerset	I-9
Souris	I-8
Sprague	I-11
Steinbach	I-11
Swan River	F-8
Teulon	H-11
The Pas	D-8
Thompson	A-10
Treherne	I-10
Tyndall	H-11
Victoria Beach	G-11
Virden	I-8
Vita	I-11
Wabowden	B-9
Warren	H-11
Wawanesa	I-9
Whitemouth	H-12
Winkler	I-10
Winnipeg	H-11
Winnipeg Beach	H-11
Winnipegosis	F-9
Woodridge	I-12

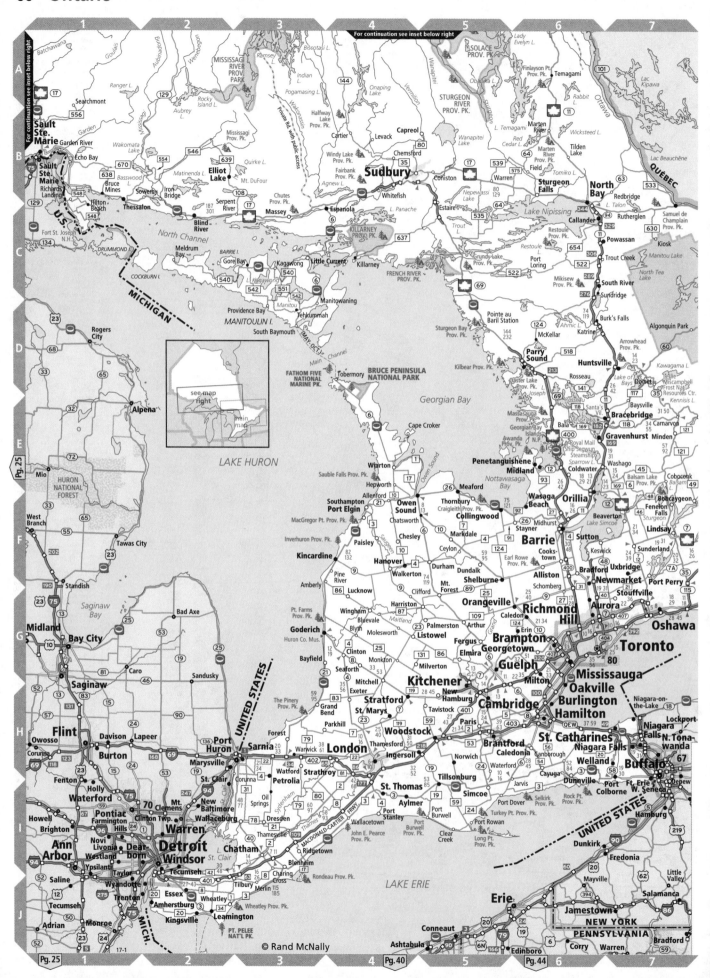

© Rand McNally

NOTE: Maps are not always in alphabetical order.
See Page 1 for map location in this atlas.

Ontario 61

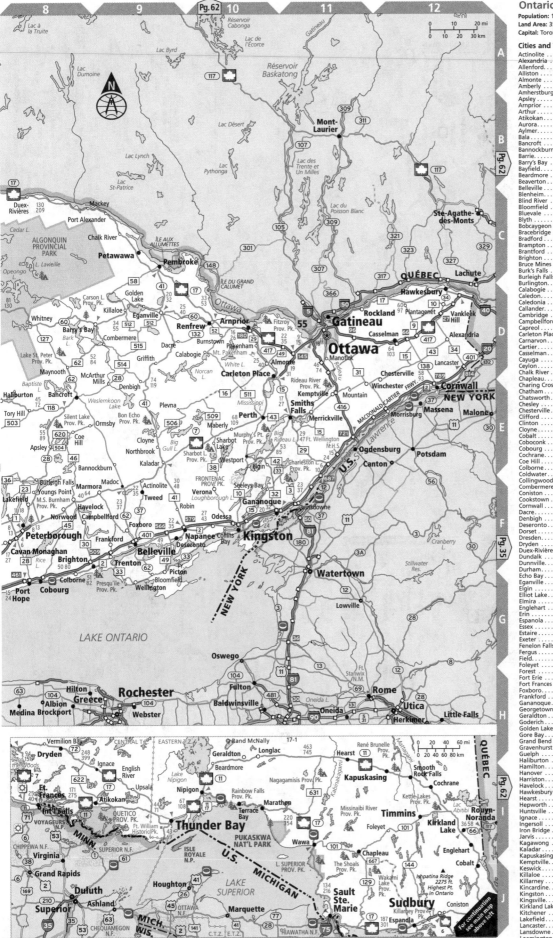

Ontario

Population: 12,851,821
Land Area: 354,342 sq. mi.
Capital: Toronto

Cities and Towns

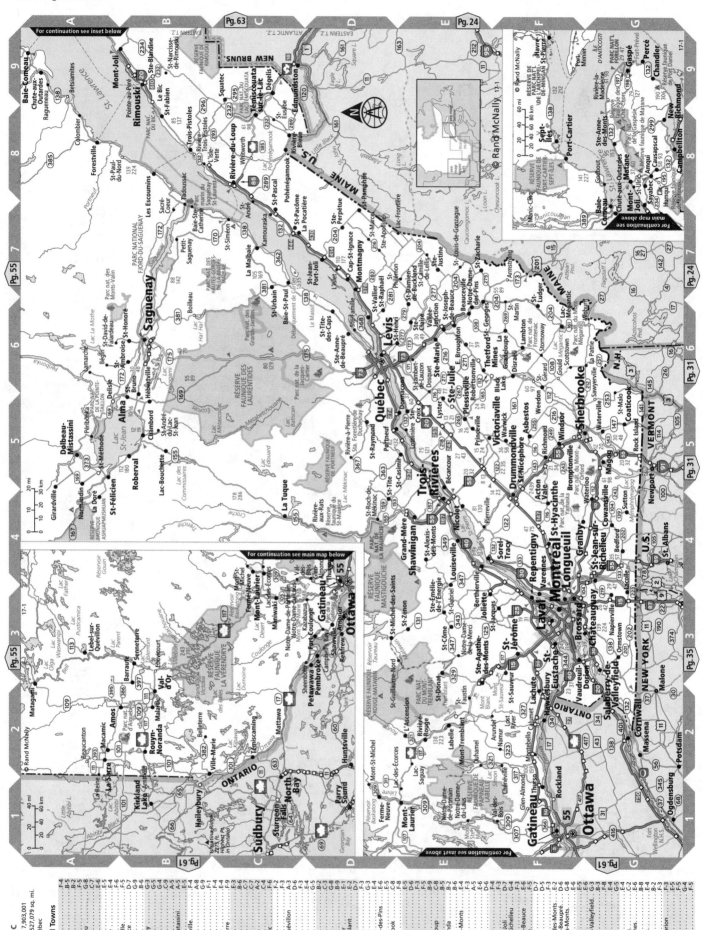

NOTE: Maps are not always in alphabetical order.
See Page 1 for map location in this atlas.

Atlantic Provinces 63

New Brunswick

Population: 751,171
Land Area: 27,587 sq. mi.
Capital: Fredericton

Cities and Towns

Bathurst	C-4
Bouctouche	D-5
Campbellton	B-3
Caraquet	B-4
Chipman	D-5
Dalhousie	B-4
Dieppe	D-5
Edmundston	C-2
Fredericton	D-3
Grand Falls (Grand Sault)	C-3
Hampton	E-4
Memramcook	D-5
Minto	D-4
Miramichi	C-4
Moncton	D-5
Oromocto	D-4
Perth-Andover	C-3
Sackville	D-5
Saint John	E-4
St. Andrews	E-3
St. Stephen	E-3
Salisbury	D-5
Shediac	D-5
Sussex	D-5
Woodstock	D-3

**Newfoundland
and Labrador**

Population: 514,536
Land Area: 144,353 sq. mi.
Capital: St. John's

Cities and Towns

Bonavista	B-9
Channel-Port aux Basques	B-7
Corner Brook	B-8
Deer Lake	B-8
Gander	B-8
Grand Falls-Windsor	B-8
Marystown	C-8
Mount Pearl	B-9
St. John's	B-9

Nova Scotia

Population: 921,727
Land Area: 20,594 sq. mi.
Capital: Halifax

Cities and Towns

Amherst	E-5
Antigonish	E-7
Bridgewater	F-5
Chester	F-5
Digby	F-4
Glace Bay	D-9
Halifax	F-6
Ingonish	C-8
Inverness	D-8
Kentville	F-5
Liverpool	G-5
Lunenburg	F-5
Middleton	F-5
New Glasgow	E-7
New Waterford	D-9
Port Hawkesbury	E-8
Shelburne	G-4
Springhill	E-5
Sydney	D-9
Sydney Mines	D-9
Truro	E-6
Windsor	F-5
Wolfville	F-5
Yarmouth	G-4

**Prince Edward
Island**

Population: 140,204
Land Area: 2,185 sq. mi.
Capital: Charlottetown

Cities and Towns

Alberton	C-5
Charlottetown	D-6
Cornwall	D-6
Georgetown	D-7
Kensington	D-6
Montague	D-7
Port Borden	D-6
Souris	D-7
Summerside	D-6
Tignish	C-6

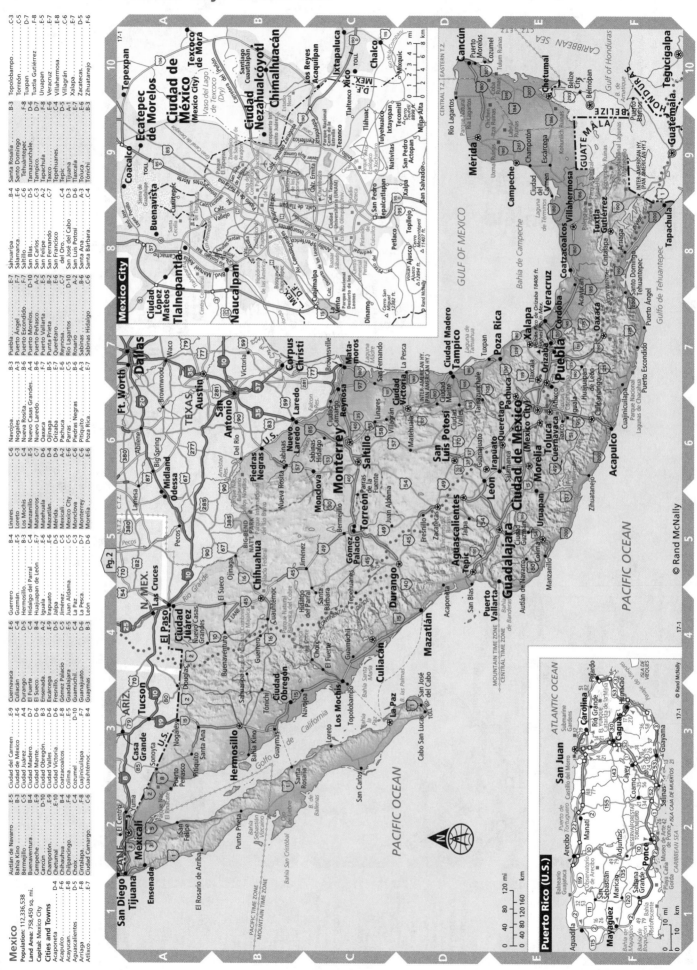

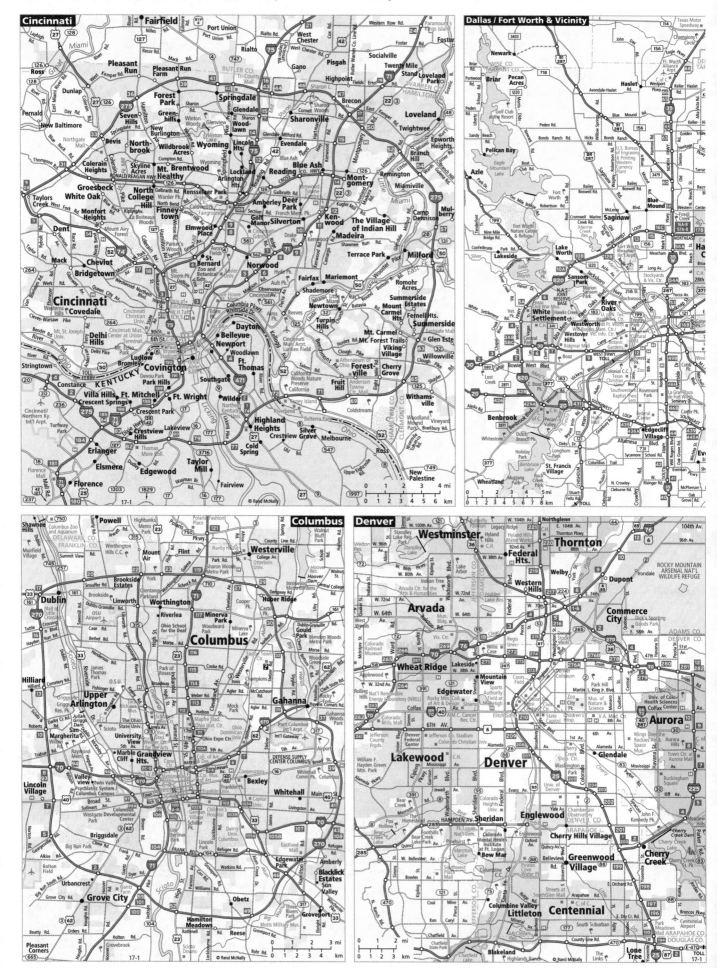

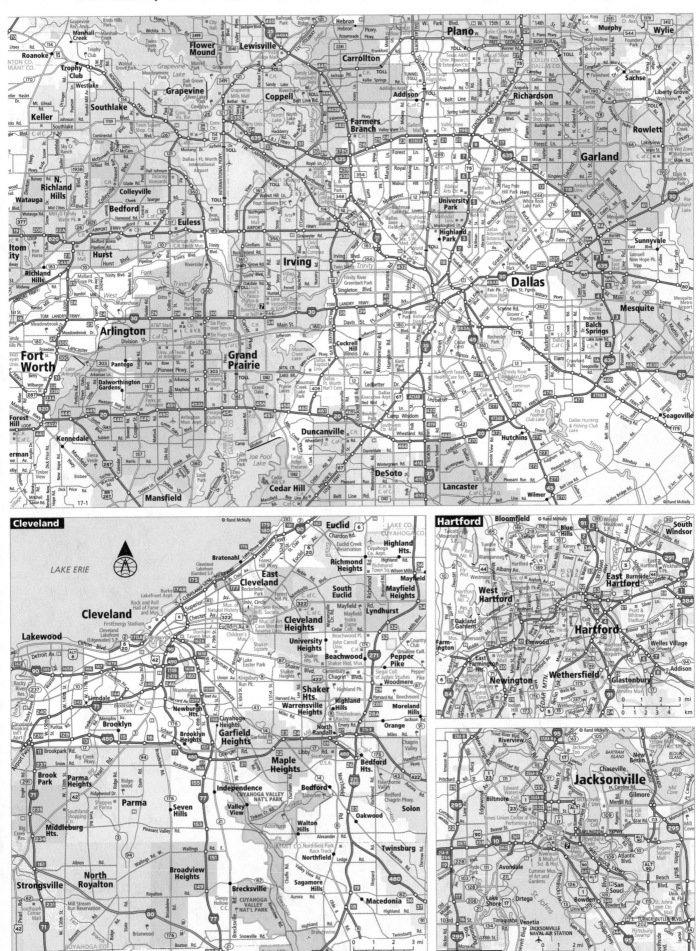

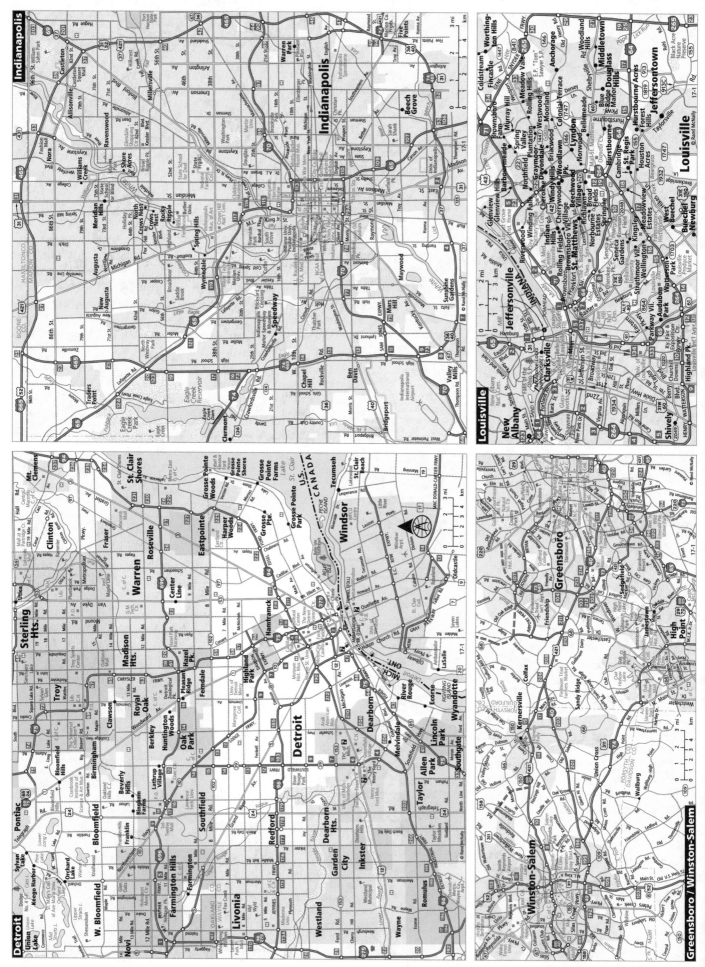

Indianapolis

Detroit

Louisville

Greensboro/Winston-Salem

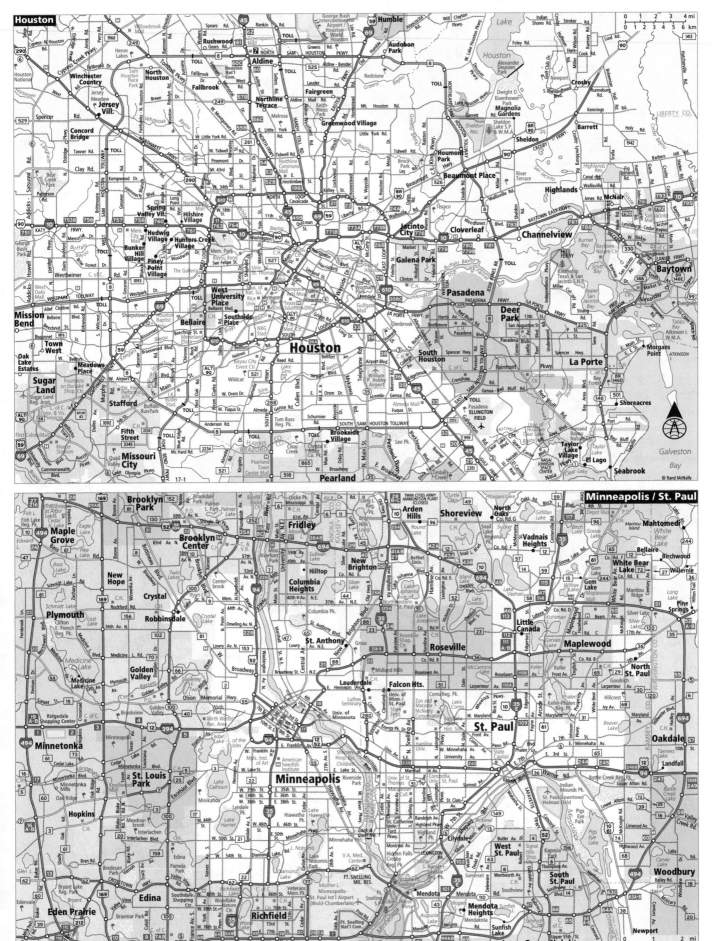

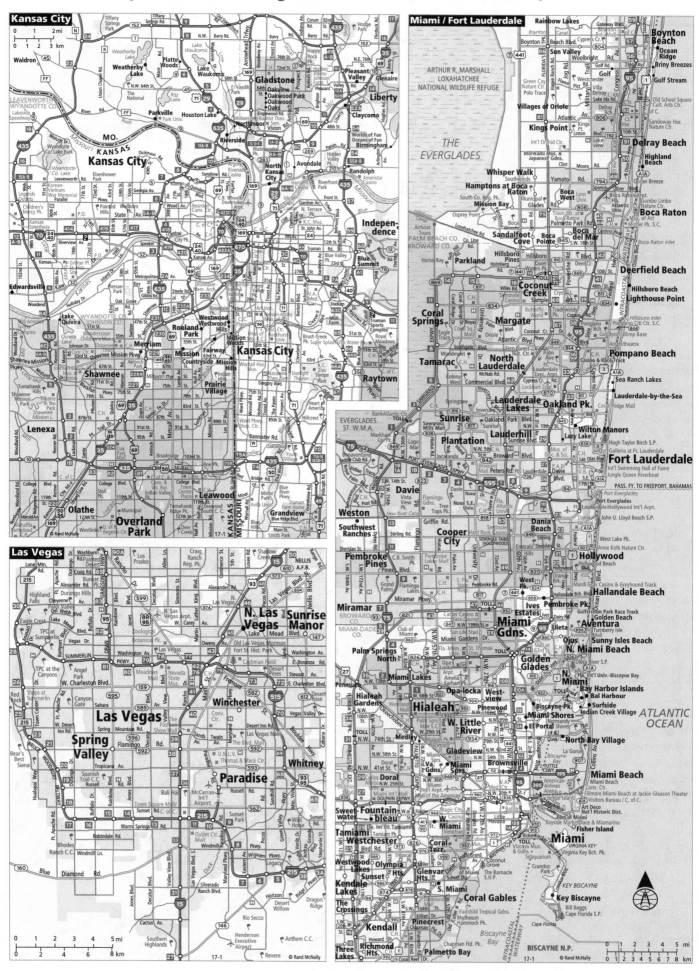

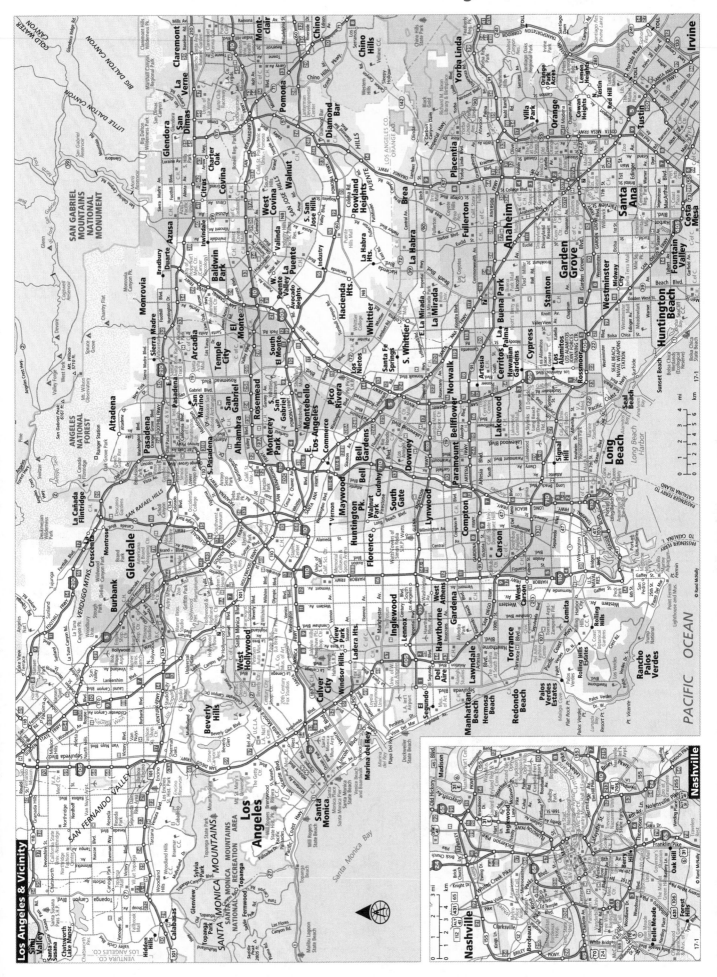

Nashville

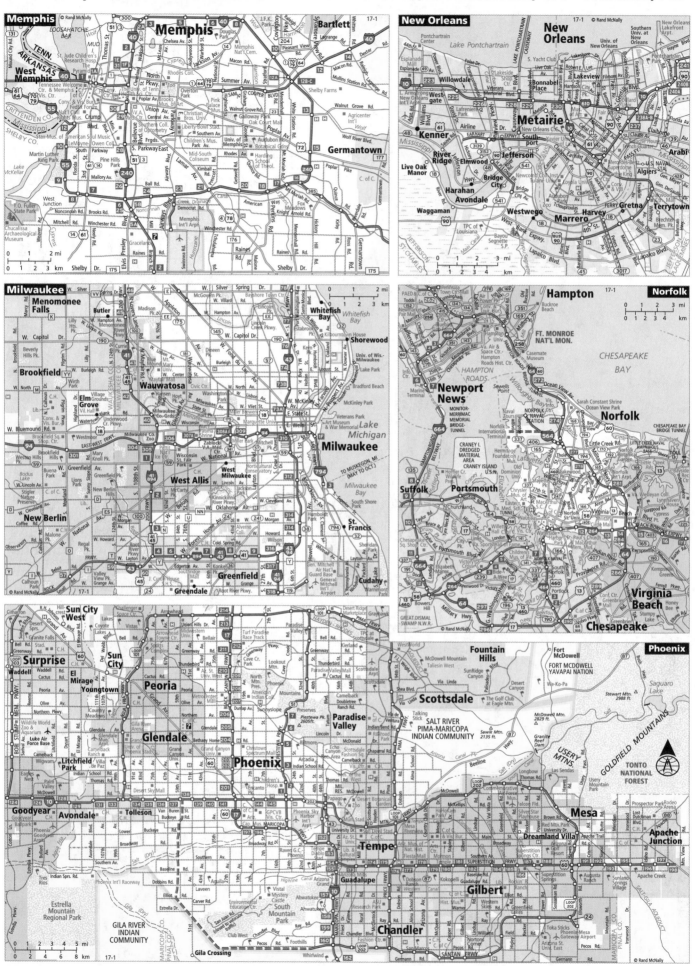

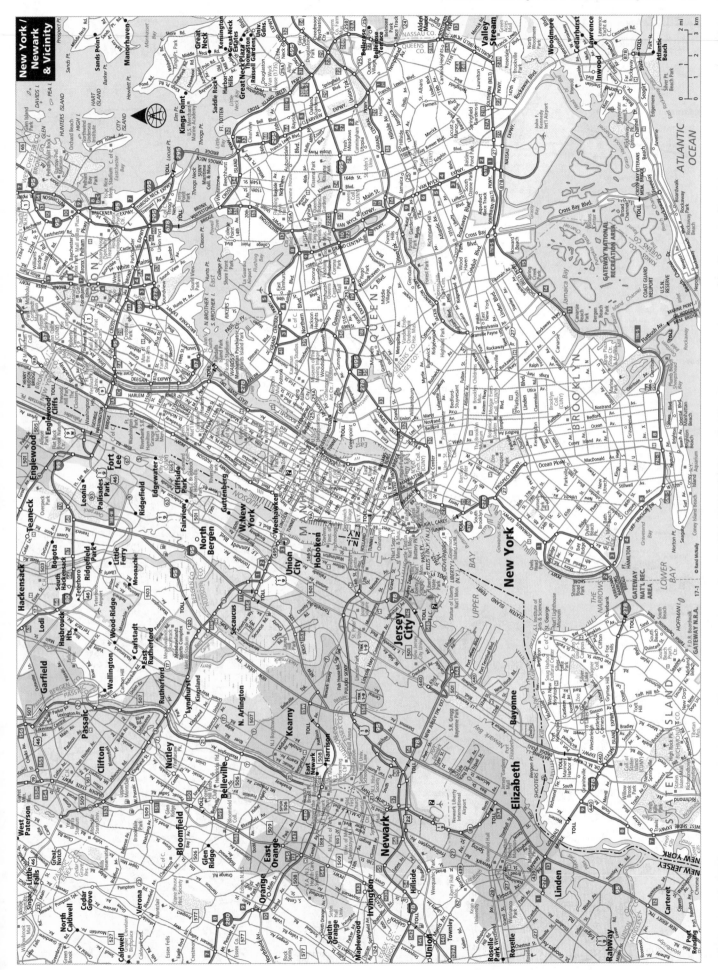

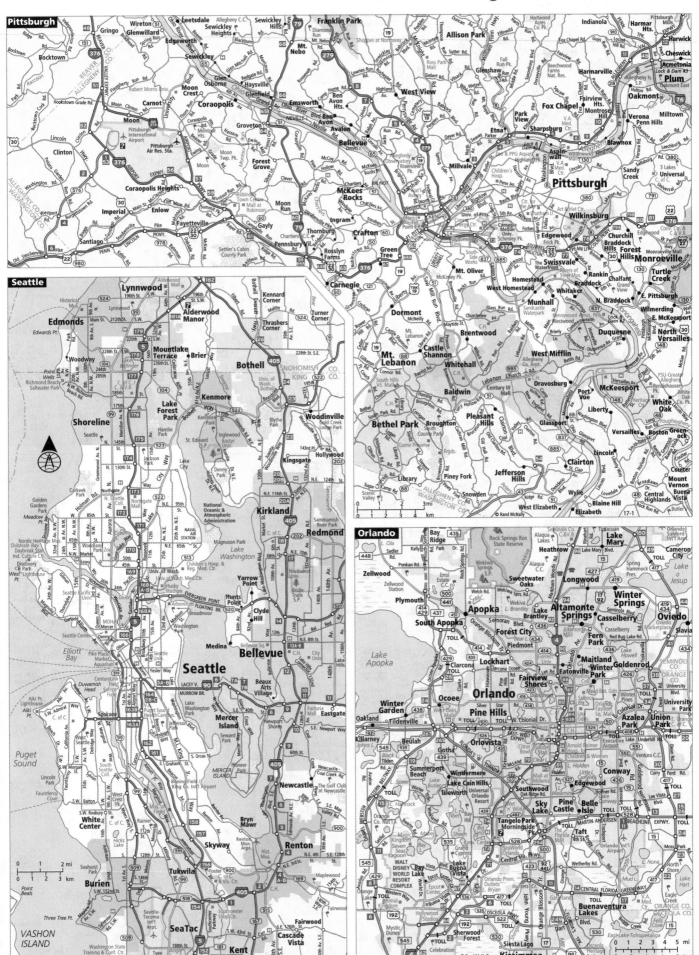

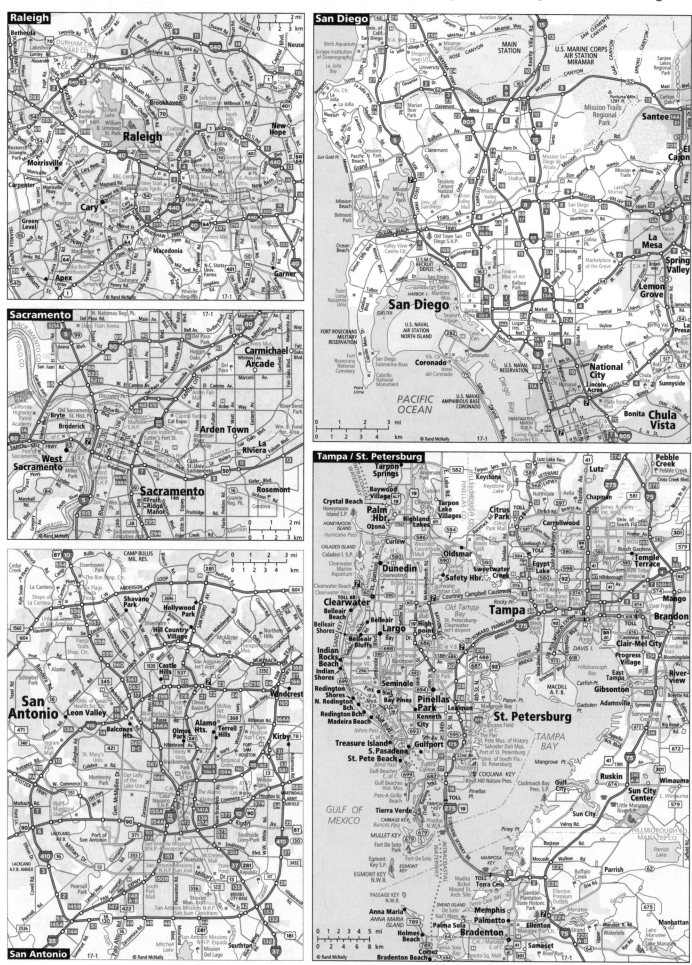

Salt Lake City

0   1   2 mi
0   1   2   3 km

San Francisco Bay Area:
San Francisco /
Oakland / San Jose

PACIFIC OCEAN

SAN FRANCISCO BAY

San Francisco · Oakland · Berkeley · Richmond · San Pablo · San Rafael · San Anselmo · Ross · Kentfield · Green Brae · Larkspur · Corte Madera · Mill Valley · Strawberry · Tiburon · Belvedere · Sausalito · Marin City · Tamalpais Valley · Almonte

Daly City · Broadmoor · Colma · Brisbane · South San Francisco · Pacifica · San Bruno · Millbrae · Burlingame · Hillsborough · San Mateo · Foster City · Belmont · San Carlos · Redwood City · Atherton · Menlo Park · Palo Alto · E. Palo Alto · Woodside · Ladera · Portola Valley · Los Altos · Los Altos Hills · Mountain View · Sunnyvale · Santa Clara · San Jose · Cupertino · Campbell · Saratoga · Los Gatos · Monte Sereno · Milpitas

Piedmont · Emeryville · Alameda · San Leandro · San Lorenzo · Ashland · Cherryland · Fairview · Castro Valley · Hayward · Union City · Newark · Fremont · Pleasanton · Dublin · San Ramon · Danville · Alamo · Diablo · Blackhawk · Camino Tassajara · Walnut Creek · Saranap · Lafayette · Orinda · Moraga · Canyon

El Cerrito · Kensington · Albany · Berkeley · El Sobrante · Sherwood Forest · Rollingwood · North Richmond · Montalvin Manor · Tara Hills · Pinole · Hercules · Rodeo · Crockett · Martinez · Pacheco · Pleasant Hill · Concord · Clayton · Pittsburg · Antioch · Vine Hill · Mountain View · Clyde

San Venetia · Santa Venetia · Los Ranchitos

Golden Gate National Recreation Area · Golden Gate Nat'l Rec. Area · Monterey Bay National Marine Sanctuary · Angel Island State Park · Mt. Diablo S.P. · Mount Diablo 3849 ft. · North Peak 3557 ft.

Salt Lake City · West Valley City · Taylorsville · Kearns · Murray · Holladay · Millcreek · S. Salt Lake · Midvale · Sandy · W. Jordan · Cottonwood Hts. · Salt Lake City Int'l Airport · Univ. of Utah · Wasatch-Cache Nat'l For. · Mt. Olympus Wilderness

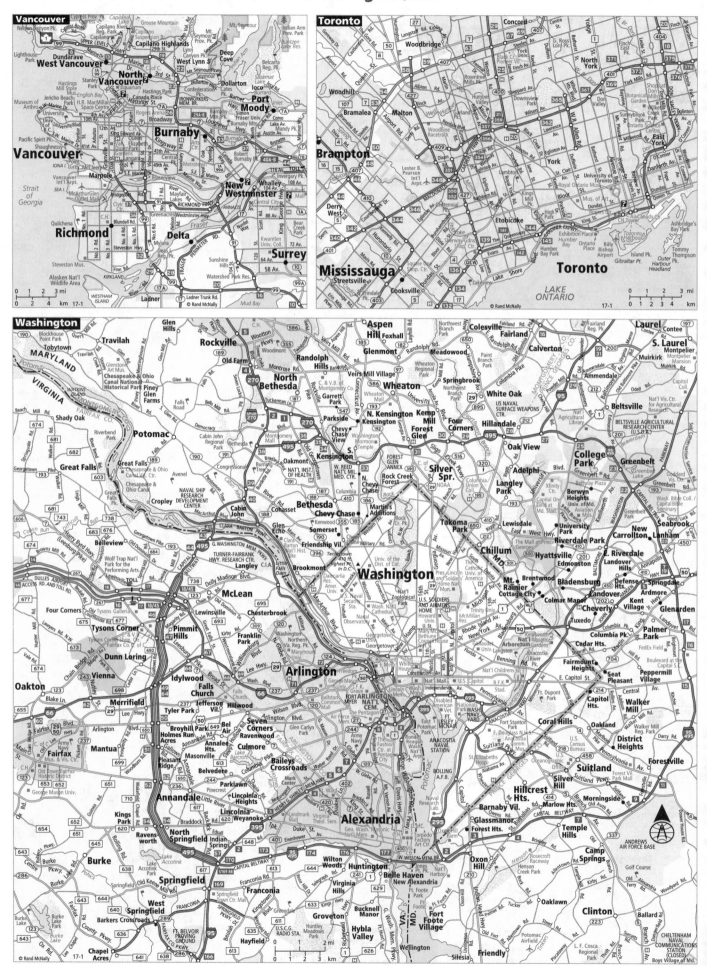

Hotel Resources

Adam's Mark Hotels & Resorts
(716) 845-5100
www.adamsmark.com

Aloft Hotels
(877) 462-5638
www.starwoodhotels.com

America's Best Inns & Suites
(800) 237-8466
americasbestinns.com

AmericInn
(800) 634-3444
www.americinn.com

Baymont Inn & Suites
(800) 337-0550
www.baymontinns.com

Best Western
(800) 780-7234
www.bestwestern.com

Budget Host
(800) 283-4678
www.budgethost.com

Clarion Hotels
(877) 424-6423
www.clarionhotel.com

Coast Hotels & Resorts
(800) 716-6199
coasthotels.com

Comfort Inn
(877) 424-6423
www.comfortinn.com

Comfort Suites
(877) 424-6423
www.comfortsuites.com

Courtyard by Marriott
(888) 236-2427
www.courtyard.com

Crowne Plaza Hotel & Resorts
(877) 227-6963
www.crowneplaza.com

Days Inn
(800) 225-3297
www.daysinn.com

Delta Hotels & Resorts
(888) 890-3222
www.deltahotels.com

Doubletree Hotels, Guest Suites, Resorts & Clubs
(800) 560-7753
doubletree3.hilton.com

Drury Hotels
(800) 378-7946
www.druryhotels.com

Econo Lodge
(877) 424-6423
www.econolodge.com

Embassy Suites Hotels
(800) 362-2779
embassysuites3.com

Extended Stay Hotels
(800) 804-3724
extendedstayamerica.com

Fairfield Inn & Suites
(888) 236-2427
fairfield.marriott.com

Fairmont Hotels & Resorts
(800) 257-7544
www.fairmont.com

Four Points by Sheraton
(800) 368-7764
www.fourpoints.com

Four Seasons
(800) 819-5053
www.fourseasons.com

Hampton Inn
(800) 445-8667
hamptoninn3.hilton.com

Hilton Hotels
(800) 445-8667
www.hilton.com

Holiday Inn Hotels & Resorts
(888) 465-4329
www.holidayinn.com

Homewood Suites
(800) 445-8667
homewoodsuites3.hilton.com

Howard Johnson
(800) 221-5801
www.hojo.com

Hyatt Hotels & Resorts
(888) 591-1234
www.hyatt.com

InterContinental Hotels & Resorts
(888) 424-6835
www.intercontinental.com

Jameson Inns
(800) 526-3766
www.jamesoninns.com

Knights Inn
(800) 477-0629
www.knightsinn.com

La Quinta Inns & Suites
(800) 753-3757
www.lq.com

Le Méridien Hotels & Resorts
(800) 543-4300
www.lemeridien.starwoodhotels.com

Loews Hotels
(800) 235-6397
www.loewshotels.com

MainStay Suites
(877) 424-6423
www.mainstaysuites.com

Marriott International
(888) 236-2427
www.marriott.com

Microtel Inns & Suites
(800) 337-0050
www.microtelinn.com

Motel 6
(800) 466-8356
www.motel6.com

Omni Hotels & Resorts
(800) 843-6664
www.omnihotels.com

Park Inn
(800) 670-7275
www.parkinn.com

Preferred Hotels & Resorts
(866) 990-9491
www.preferredhotels.com

Quality Inn & Suites
(877) 424-6423
www.qualityinn.com

Radisson
(800) 967-9033
www.radisson.com

Ramada Worldwide
(800) 854-9517
www.ramada.com

Red Lion Hotels
(800) 733-5466
www.redlion.com

Red Roof Inn
(800) 733-7663
www.redroof.com

Renaissance Hotels
(888) 236-2427
www.renaissancehotels.com

Residence Inn by Marriott
(888) 236-2427
www.residenceinn.com

The Ritz-Carlton
(800) 542-8680
www.ritzcarlton.com

Rodeway Inn
(877) 424-6423
www.rodewayinn.com

Sheraton Hotels & Resorts
(800) 325-3535
www.sheraton.com

Sleep Inn
(877) 424-6423
www.sleepinn.com

Super 8
(800) 454-3213
www.super8.com

Travelodge Hotels
(800) 525-4055
www.travelodge.com

Westin Hotels & Resorts
(800) 937-8461
www.westin.starwoodhotels.com

Wyndham Hotels & Resorts
(877) 999-3223
www.wyndham.com

NOTE: All toll-free reservation numbers are for the U.S. and Canada unless otherwise noted. These numbers were accurate at press time, but are subject to change.

Mileage Chart

This handy chart offers more than 2,400 mileages covering 77 North American cities. Want more mileages? Visit **randmcnally.com/MC** and type in any two cities or addresses.

Mileages in this chart are based upon the routes usually followed by motorists. Highway systems include interstate, U.S., and state highways.

Mileages ©RM Acquisition, LLC d/b/a Rand McNally

	Albuquerque, NM	Atlanta, GA	Billings, MT	Boston, MA	Charlotte, NC	Chicago, IL	Cincinnati, OH	Dallas, TX	Denver, CO	Detroit, MI	Houston, TX	Indianapolis, IN	Kansas City, MO	Los Angeles, CA	Memphis, TN	Miami, FL	Milwaukee, WI	Minneapolis, MN	New Orleans, LA	New York, NY	Omaha, NE	Orlando, FL	Philadelphia, PA	Phoenix, AZ	Pittsburgh, PA	Portland, OR	St. Louis, MO	Salt Lake City, UT	San Francisco, CA	Seattle, WA	Washington, DC	Wichita, KS
Albuquerque, NM		1386	998	2219	1626	1333	1387	647	446	1570	884	1279	784	786	1008	1952	1354	1225	1165	2001	863	1730	1924	425	1641	1363	1037	599	1086	1438	1885	591
Amarillo, TX	288	1102	965	1935	1342	1049	1103	363	424	1286	589	995	570	1072	720	1668	1132	1009	881	1716	647	1446	1640	746	1357	1669	752	883	1370	1743	1600	418
Atlanta, GA	1386		1831	1095	244	715	461	780	1404	722	794	533	800	2174	379	661	809	1127	468	882	992	440	780	1844	684	2603	555	1878	2472	2649	637	955
Atlantic City, NJ	1985	831	2072	338	590	818	632	1518	1792	644	1598	703	1187	2774	1063	1248	910	1232	1273	126	1272	1038	60	2447	365	2922	948	2201	2934	2889	188	1379
Austin, TX	705	920	1495	1959	1164	1121	1128	196	950	1358	163	1067	702	1381	643	1341	1204	1136	503	1737	839	1124	1658	1010	1411	2068	825	1304	1760	2143	1524	542
Baltimore, MD	1887	683	1953	400	442	699	513	1368	1673	524	1448	584	1068	2670	914	1082	792	1112	1124	192	1153	889	97	2349	246	2804	829	2081	2816	2771	39	1260
Billings, MT	998	1831		2236	1990	1246	1546	1425	551	1535	1652	1435	1026	1240	1477	2497	1173	838	1868	2041	845	2275	2011	1210	1713	891	1278	552	1173	818	1951	1064
Birmingham, AL	1241	146	1780	1177	390	660	466	636	1329	724	668	478	749	2030	233	746	754	1072	341	960	939	534	880	1700	748	2551	502	1826	2327	2598	745	810
Boise, ID	938	2177	621	2660	2336	1693	1943	1702	830	1960	1930	1835	1372	842	1825	2844	1732	1461	2216	2465	1225	2622	2435	914	2137	431	1622	340	639	513	1338
Boston, MA	2219	1095	2236		841	983	870	1764	1970	724	1844	937	1421	2983	1312	1482	1074	1396	1520	216	1436	1288	306	2681	570	3086	1182	2663	3098	3054	439	1613
Branson, MO	864	652	1241	1433	868	545	601	435	806	784	602	493	209	1651	274	1284	630	643	597	1201	402	1062	1138	1326	851	2013	249	1288	1950	2060	1081	292
Calgary, AB	1542	2357	552	2615	2400	1627	1925	1967	1096	1916	2209	1814	1567	1557	2028	3018	1555	1221	2419	2439	1387	2797	2391	1524	2093	787	1820	869	1500	678	2334	1606
Charleston, SC	1703	319	2133	970	209	908	620	1099	1706	826	1105	726	1103	2491	696	583	1002	1324	742	768	1294	380	668	2165	654	2904	857	2180	2789	2951	532	1272
Charlotte, NC	1626	244	1990	841		769	477	1023	1566	616	1038	583	961	2414	619	728	867	1180	712	641	1151	526	539	2088	446	2761	714	2037	2712	2808	398	1092
Chicago, IL	1333	715	1246	983	769		289	926	1002	282	1085	181	526	2015	531	1381	90	408	923	787	470	1153	757	1795	459	2118	295	1398	2130	2063	697	724
Cincinnati, OH	1387	461	1546	870	477	289		934	1187	259	1055	109	584	2172	482	1127	381	703	804	637	722	905	571	1849	288	2369	348	1647	2380	2363	512	779
Cleveland, OH	1598	714	1597	638	514	344	248	1194	1330	169	1315	315	799	2342	729	1240	434	756	1057	460	797	1043	428	2060	134	2446	560	1725	2458	2414	370	992
Columbus, OH	1457	567	1606	763	426	354	107	1039	1261	212	1174	189	657	2244	587	1164	445	766	910	533	792	954	468	1920	174	2439	421	1718	2451	2425	411	851
Corpus Christi, TX	855	1001	1622	2051	1244	1338	1262	410	1077	1542	207	1228	919	1494	782	1394	1421	1353	554	1844	1056	1172	1754	1121	1561	2218	1042	1454	1873	2292	1619	758
Dallas, TX	647	780	1425	1764	1023	926	934		880	1163	239	873	489	1437	453	1307	1010	928	519	1548	656	1086	1467	1066	1221	2128	630	1403	1734	2193	1332	361
Denver, CO	446	1404	551	1970	1566	1002	1187	880		1270	1035	1083	603	1015	1097	2069	1042	913	1398	1775	534	1851	1732	908	1447	1256	854	533	1268	1320	1671	519
Des Moines, IA	983	902	946	1299	1057	335	580	683	670	599	938	474	194	1682	617	1563	375	244	1008	1105	135	1339	1074	1445	777	1786	350	1065	1798	1764	1015	391
Detroit, MI	1570	722	1535	724	616	282	259	1163	1270		1319	277	764	2281	742	1354	374	696	1066	613	736	1144	583	2032	285	2385	533	1664	2397	2353	522	964
Duluth, MN	1375	1187	860	1370	1239	466	760	1092	1063	754	1331	651	586	2076	963	1852	394	152	1354	1264	530	1632	1230	1838	932	1749	679	1458	2033	1677	1171	785
Edmonton, AB	1724	2391	722	2549	2443	1670	1968	2149	1278	1958	2391	1857	1626	1755	2147	3058	1598	1264	2538	2482	1445	2836	2434	1721	2136	966	1878	1069	1695	793	2377	1787
El Paso, TX	266	1418	1257	2373	1662	1455	1569	635	707	1702	744	1398	929	796	1089	1934	1497	1377	1095	2202	1004	1712	2102	424	1774	1630	1157	866	1175	1705	1967	730
Fargo, ND	1318	1361	607	1629	1414	641	937	1079	873	930	1321	825	600	1848	1054	2205	569	234	1445	1438	420	1807	1405	1780	1107	1497	841	1160	1781	1424	1348	685
Gatlinburg, TN	1439	196	1803	922	202	578	290	884	1376	552	964	396	773	2226	431	865	672	994	640	707	964	640	625	1901	493	2574	527	1850	2525	2621	490	905
Guadalajara, JA	1194	1739	2194	2789	1982	1954	1962	1028	1639	2191	948	1901	1535	1501	1482	2131	2037	1969	1292	2592	1672	1910	2492	1212	2261	2545	1658	1792	1963	2631	2356	1377
Gulfport, MS	1221	399	1912	1482	643	896	767	562	1386	1025	403	780	883	1949	365	792	988	1196	78	1266	1073	572	1180	1577	1052	2633	647	1909	2307	2730	1036	867
Houston, TX	884	794	1652	1844	1038	1085	1055	239	1035	1319		1021	732	1550	575	1186	1163	1171	348	1632	898	965	1547	1178	1354	2356	784	1634	1929	2431	1411	595
Indianapolis, IN	1279	533	1435	937	583	181	109	873	1083	277	1021		482	2068	464	1198	272	591	818	707	613	968	643	1742	359	2260	243	1541	2273	2253	582	674
Jacksonville, FL	1636	346	2183	1146	379	1068	796	992	1756	1002	871	874	1152	2421	677	349	1163	1474	547	939	1344	141	844	2050	825	2954	907	2232	2723	3001	706	1272
Kansas City, MO	784	800	1026	1421	961	526	584	489	603	764	732	482		1616	451	1466	565	436	844	1196	184	1246	1127	1246	840	1797	248	1073	1808	1844	1066	198
Key West, FL	2099	809	2646	1659	886	1534	1275	1455	2222	1515	1334	1348	1617	2884	1159	160	1632	1944	1010	1446	1807	387	1357	2514	1332	3417	1370	2693	3186	3464	1213	1735
Las Vegas, NV	572	1959	973	2714	2199	1746	1932	1220	747	2013	1457	1828	1349	270	1661	2525	1786	1656	1739	2518	1278	2303	2480	285	2190	1023	1600	419	569	1128	2428	1164
Lexington, KY	1371	369	1610	917	400	370	83	876	1186	344	996	184	581	2158	423	1030	464	782	745	701	771	817	638	1833	370	2381	334	1657	2392	2428	533	773
Little Rock, AR	877	515	1407	1447	754	650	617	319	965	885	439	583	381	1666	136	1147	724	815	425	1230	574	925	1150	1340	905	2211	345	1488	1963	2275	1015	446
Los Angeles, CA	786	2174	1240	2983	2414	2015	2172	1437	1015	2281	1550	2068	1616		1794	2735	2055	1925	1894	2787	1546	2515	2713	370	2428	963	1821	688	380	1134	2670	1377
Memphis, TN	1008	379	1471	1312	619	531	482	453	1097	742	575	464	451	1794		1012	622	831	394	1094	641	778	1014	1471	768	2245	283	1524	2095	2299	879	577
Mexico City, DF	1404	1718	2301	2768	1962	2017	1990	1756	2254	924	1963	1598	1839	1500	2111	2100	2032	1272	2511	1735	1889	2771	1469	2279	2768	1721	2003	2218	2842	2336	1440	
Miami, FL	1952	661	2497	1482	728	1381	1127	1307	1854	1186	1198	1466	2735	1012	1475		1791	861	1288	1658	235	1180	2362	1173	3260	1173	3315	1044	1587			
Milwaukee, WI	1354	809	1173	1074	867	90	381	1010	1042	374	1163	272	565	2055	622	1475		337	1015	879	509	1258	849	1817	551	2062	379	1437	2170	1990	788	763
Minneapolis, MN	1225	1127	838	1396	1180	408	703	928	913	696	1171	591	436	1925	831	1791	337		1223	1204	372	1573	1171	1687	874	1727	563	1308	2040	1655	1110	634
Mobile, AL	1234	328	1874	1427	571	917	721	589	1414	978	468	737	850	2014	382	719	1011	1224	144	1202	1038	497	1101	1643	1000	2661	645	1936	2320	2727	965	894
Montréal, QC	2129	1218	2099	310	980	847	824	1722	1832	560	1884	847	1330	2845	1314	1647	938	1262	1643	382	1302	1437	454	2591	603	2948	1092	2228	2960	2916	587	1529
Nashville, TN	1219	248	1586	1099	408	469	273	664	1158	534	786	287	555	2006	209	913	564	881	532	884	747	692	802	1682	560	2357	307	1633	2306	2404	667	668
New Orleans, LA	1165	468	1868	1520	712	923	804	519	1398	1066	348	818	844	1894	394	861	1015	1223		1304	1032	641	1222	1523	1090	2642	675	1920	2252	2716	1087	880
New York, NY	2001	882	2041	216	787	637	1548	1775	2163	1632	707	1196	2787	1094	1288	879	1204	1304		1245	1089	95	2463	369	2170	2902	2858	228	1391			
Norfolk, VA	1910	558	2132	569	328	878	605	1350	1758	704	1362	720	1155	2707	898	950	969	1295	1030	370	1335	755	271	2373	425	2962	911	2238	2973	2949	193	1349
Oklahoma City, OK	542	844	1203	1678	1084	792	846	206	631	1029	437	739	347	1326	466	1476	876	788	722	1460	452	1254	1384	1005	1101	1922	496	1200	1627	1948	1344	160
Omaha, NE	863	992	845	1436	1151	470	722	656	534	736	898	613	184	1546	641	1658	509	372	1032	1245		1436	1212	1325	914	1650	439	930	1662	1663	1151	298
Orlando, FL	1730	440	2275	1288	526	1153	905	1086	1851	1144	965	968	1246	2515	778	235	1258	1573	641	1089	1436		986	2145	975	3048	999	2323	2816	3093	849	1265
Ottawa, ON	2039	1158	1768	428	920	760	732	1632	1748	471	1804	757	1240	2763	1230	1618	859	1032	1582	440	1213	1408	447	2501	546	2660	1002	2142	2877	2586	566	1439
Philadelphia, PA	1924	780	2011	306	539	757	571	1467	1732	583	1547	643	1127	2713	1014	1180	849	1171	1222	95	1212	986		2387	305	2861	888	2140	2873	2828	137	1319
Phoenix, AZ	425	1844	1210	2681	2088	1795	1849	1066	908	2032	1178	1742	1246	373	1471	2362	1817	1687	1523	2463	1325	2145	2387		2104	1332	1499	653	749	1414	2348	1053
Pittsburgh, PA	1641	684	1713	570	446	459	288	1221	1447	285	1354	359	840	2428	768	1173	551	874	1090	369	914	975	305	2104		2563	604	1842	2574	2530	243	1035
Portland, ME	2315	1192	2333	107	938	1079	967	1861	2067	825	1940	1034	1518	3082	1408	1585	1176	1492	1616	304	1533	1385	402	2778	666	3186	1279	2461	3196	3151	535	1710
Portland, OR	1363	2603	830	2761	2118	2369	2128	1256	2385	2356	2260	1797	1650	963	2062	2891	1650	1332	2642	2891	1332	3048	2861	1332	2563		2050	765	635	174	2800	1764
Rapid City, SD	843	1508	323	1900	1670	912	1208	1061	392	1200	1291	1100	704	1312	1160	2173	840	575	1551	1708	525	1956	1675	1305	1378	1215	959	649	1384	1142	1618	699
Reno, NV	1019	2396	958	2881	2555	1913	2163	1668	1051	2180	1904	2056	1591	470	2029	3063	1953	1818	2186	2685	1445	2841	2656	733	2357	578	1844	518	218	720	2595	1558
Richmond, VA	1832	532	2051	547	293	797	512	1278	1671	622	1329	627	1069	2620	824	944	888	1210	1002	334	1259	742	245	2294	344	2869	822	2145	2880	2868	108	1261
St. Louis, MO	1037	555	1278	1182	714	295	348	630	854	533	784	243	248	1821	284	1221	379	563	675	954	439	999	888	1499	604	2050		1326	2061	2096	827	442
Salt Lake City, UT	599	1878	552	2365	2037	1398	1647	1403	533	1664	1634	1541	1073	688	1524	2437	1330	1210	2323	2140	653	1842	765	1326	735	839	2079		2079	1042		
San Antonio, TX	712	986	1480	2039	1230	1202	1210	276	935	1439	195	1149	766	1357	727	1379	1285	1205	541	1822	920	1160	1742	985	1495	2076	906	1311	1736	2150	1607	625
San Diego, CA	810	2138	1302	3046	2381	2080	2196	1359	1077	2346	1472	2089	1597	120	1819	2656	2118	1986	1816	2809	1613	2436	2738	355	2452	1083	1845	750	501	1256	2693	1401
San Francisco, CA	1086	2472	1173	3098	2712	2130	2380	1734	1268	2397	1929	2273	1808	382	2095	3038	2170	2040	2252	2902	1662	2816	2873	749	2574	635	2061	735		807	2812	1775
Santa Fe, NM	58	1379	943	2212	1618	1313	1379	640	391	1562	877	1272	766	846	998	1944	1336	1207	1158	1994	891	1723	1917	520	1634	1388	1029	625	1144	1463	1879	572
Sault Ste. Marie, ON	1777	1040	1273	923	947	483	577	1370	1428	348	1527	540	951	2465	972	1685	400	545	1355	921	850	1475	911	2240	614	2166	740	1848	2581	2090	854	1150
Seattle, WA	1438	2649	818	3054	2808	2063	2363	2193	1300	2353	2431	2253	1844	1134	2299	3315	1990	1655	2716	2858	1663	3093	2828	1414	2530	174	2096	839	807		2768	1828
Spokane, WA	1320	2369	541	2774	2528	1785	2084	1964	1091	2075	2192	1973	1564	1216	2018	3035	1712	1377	2409	2580	1383	2814	2550	1381	2252	352	1817	720	874	279	2490	1600
Tampa, FL	1746	451	2293	1342	578	1166	916	1102	1860	1178	980	984	1252	2525	779	280	1260	1578	651	1138	1445	85	1040	2153	1023	3064	1008	2340	2832	3111	904	1381
Toronto, ON	1800	963	1771	548	756	529	493	1393	1504	231	1551	518	1001	2517	983	1488	609	933	1306	489	974	1284	497	2262	316	2620	763	1899	2632	2588	486	1188
Tulsa, OK	645	782	1234	1576	1022	687	738	258	692	927	487	635	263	1433	402	1414	773	704	671	1330	380	1192	1287	1100	994	1938	392	1215	1731	2012	1234	174
Vancouver, BC	1575	2785	953	3188	2944	2198	2499	2338	1465	2487	2565	2389	1980	1275	2437	3451	2125	1790	2851	2993	1799	3229	2963	1550	2665	313	2232	973	947	141	2903	1973
Washington, DC	1885	637	1951	439	398	697	512	1332	1671	522	1411	582	1066	2670	879	1044	788	1110	1087	228	1151	849	137	2348	244	2800	827	2079	2812	2768		1258
Wichita, KS	591	955	1064	1613	1092	724	779	361	519	964	595	674	198	1377	577	1587	763	634	880	1391	298	1365	1319	1053	1035	1764	442	1042	1775	1828	1258	